The FINEST PLACE WE KNOW

The FINEST PLACE WE KNOW

A CENTENNIAL HISTORY OF MURRAY STATE UNIVERSITY, 1922–2022

ROBERT L JACKSON, SEAN J. McLAUGHLIN, *and* SARAH MARIE OWENS

UNIVERSITY PRESS OF KENTUCKY

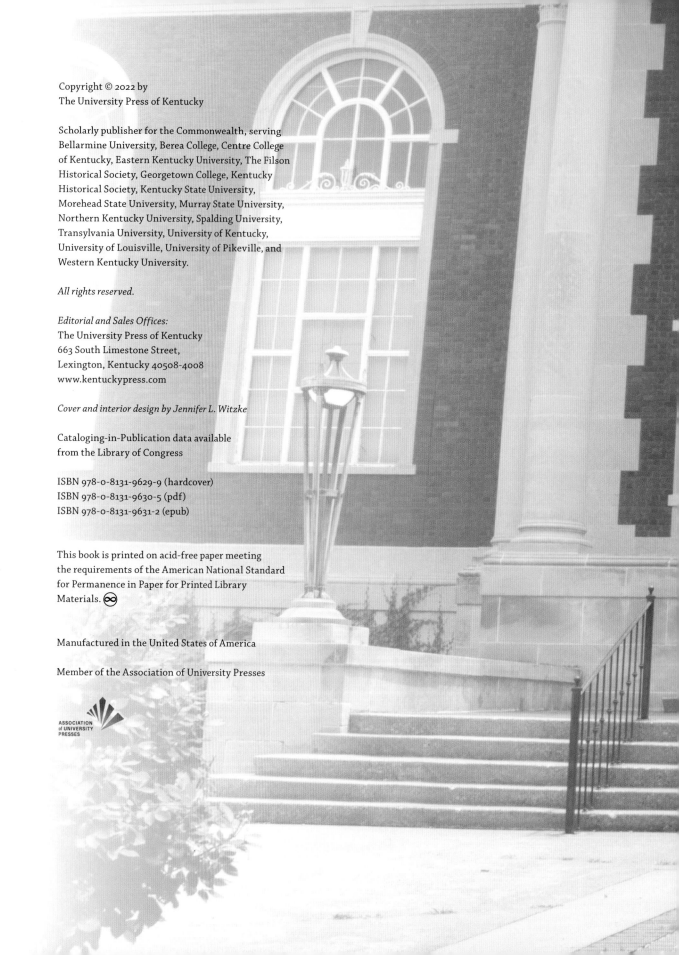

Copyright © 2022 by
The University Press of Kentucky

Scholarly publisher for the Commonwealth, serving
Bellarmine University, Berea College, Centre College
of Kentucky, Eastern Kentucky University, The Filson
Historical Society, Georgetown College, Kentucky
Historical Society, Kentucky State University,
Morehead State University, Murray State University,
Northern Kentucky University, Spalding University,
Transylvania University, University of Kentucky,
University of Louisville, University of Pikeville, and
Western Kentucky University.

Editorial and Sales Offices:
The University Press of Kentucky
663 South Limestone Street,
Lexington, Kentucky 40508-4008
www.kentuckypress.com

Cover and interior design by Jennifer L. Witzke

Cataloging-in-Publication data available
from the Library of Congress

ISBN 978-0-8131-9629-9 (hardcover)
ISBN 978-0-8131-9630-5 (pdf)
ISBN 978-0-8131-9631-2 (epub)

This book is printed on acid-free paper meeting
the requirements of the American National Standard
for Permanence in Paper for Printed Library
Materials. ∞

Manufactured in the United States of America

Member of the Association of University Presses

ASSOCIATION
of UNIVERSITY
PRESSES

THE FOUNDER
RAINEY T. WELLS

CONTENTS

Preface   *x*

1   **The Founding Era** | *1922–1936*   2

2   **Surviving Hard Times** | *1936–1948*   28

3   **The Postwar Boom** | *1948–1966*   42

4   **The Boomers Come of Age** | *1966–1981*   54

5   **Innovation and Modernization** | *1981–1997*   70

6   **A New Millennium** | *1997–2013*   90

7   **Preparing for a New Racer Century** | *2013–present*   122

    Epilogue   160

    Appendix: Murray State University Leadership   163

    Index   169

PREFACE

As we started working on this book project in 2019, pre-pandemic as we now say, I reflected on a book I read several years ago, *Inside Stories,* and specifically a poignant chapter written by Dr. Joel Spring. Spring stated, "We are our histories. What we think, what we believe in, and the choices we make are products of our histories. And, of course, our personal histories are embedded in the history of the arts, institutions and governments." My wife, Karen, our family, and I have walked these grounds and have been touched by this special place along with nearly 80,000 other alumni, students, faculty, staff, and others. Murray State University is forever embedded in all of us.

Our early years were well-documented in Dr. Ralph H. Woods's 1972 book, *Fifty Years of Progress.* Additionally, I am very grateful to Dr. Kern Alexander's excellent compilation, research, and editing of Dr. John W. Carr's papers outlining our early history. Our goal with this book, primarily a pictorial history, was to ensure we recorded our growth and development of the past 100 years, celebrating our centennial and recognizing our achievements. Murray State University, like all institutions of higher learning, has a unique and important history that needs to be well documented for future generations.

While beginning this manuscript, I often wondered if our founder, Dr. Rainey T. Wells, and first president, Dr. John W. Carr, ever envisioned that their small, rural normal school, started in a local high school, would evolve over 100 years later into a nationally recognized comprehensive university offering 145 degree programs, a campus comprising nearly 200 buildings on over 1,700 acres of university and Murray State University Foundation properties, students from 49 countries and nearly every state, and approximately 80,000 alumni. It would have been nearly impossible to imagine this growth and transformative change from the confines of those original classrooms in our first building, now Wrather Hall, as our university was being planned.

During the past 100 years, we have been blessed with extraordinary leadership as we faced each chapter of our development; from the perseverance of Dr. Rainey T. Wells to achieve the near-impossible feat of securing a new normal school, to the resilience needed in order to survive early state and national struggles, to the determined spirit that we possess today. The three stars emblazoned on our shield symbolize these efforts: Hope, Endeavor, and Achievement.

Furthermore, the many hurdles throughout our country's and state's history, including the Great Depression, World War II, funding challenges, and a global pandemic, among numerous other pressures, have caused the university to always emerge stronger and better focused. This is a credit to our past and present students, faculty, staff, administrators, presidents, regents, foundation trustees, alumni, friends, and thousands of donors, all of whom played and continue to play a key role in advancing our university.

Dr. John W. Carr stated in an April 1, 1926, letter to the board of regents, "The work of this institution has only begun. . . . I want to see this faculty continue to develop in not only teaching ability, but heart power—the ability to lead and inspire. . . . I want to see the fullest opportunities furnished to students . . . and [for them] to express themselves in science, art, music, literature, play, work, religion and especially in the teaching of children. . . . I want to see young men and women who will become effective leaders. . . . I want to see all of these things and more." These visionary statements are still true today and continue to inspire our work 100 years later. And, as I state often, our best days are ahead of us.

This book, *The Finest Place We Know: A Centennial History of Murray State University,* outlines our first 100 years in pictures and text, denoting our tremendous growth and change from our humble beginnings. It is broken into significant periods in our history to better portray the many changes and improvements that occurred in each.

Dr. Robert L Jackson and Karen Jackson, Oakhurst.

Importantly, I am grateful to everyone who has played a role in publishing this book in order that future generations know our history. Special thanks go to the University Press of Kentucky; to our talented professionals in Pogue Library; to the co-chairs of this project and senior editorial committee: Cris Ferguson, interim dean of University Libraries; Jordan Smith, executive director of governmental and institutional relations; Jill Hunt, senior executive coordinator for the president and coordinator for board relations; Cami Duffy, executive director of institutional diversity, equity and access; Carrie McGinnis, director of alumni relations; to the Centennial Book Committee members; to Lacy Risner, graduate student; and to the authors: myself, Dr. Sean J. McLaughlin, special collections and exhibits director, and Sarah Marie Owens, library specialist, who spent months of researching, writing, and editing to ensure its completion. All of these individuals and others made this project a reality.

Lastly, as we look forward, I am confident that our next century will bring the same Racer Spirit, determination, and perseverance as we address a new set of challenges and opportunities. As Dean A. B. Austin stated in our alma mater, "*In the heart of Jackson's Purchase, 'neath the sun's warm glow, is the home of Murray State, the finest place we know.*"

We hope you enjoy this journey through our history.

Dr. Bob Jackson, '85
President

The FINEST PLACE WE KNOW

| 1 |

The Founding Era

1922–1936

Introduction

A T THE DAWN OF THE AUTOMOBILE AGE, MURRAY was a pleasant county seat of a little over 2,000 people, the sort of tight-knit place where everyone knew their neighbors. There were plenty of small businesses on the court square, along with train service to Paducah and Paris, Tennessee, but ours was not the biggest or busiest town in the Purchase Area at the time. It did, however, have one crucial asset that set it apart: an extremely savvy civic booster and longtime champion of higher education, Rainey T. Wells.

Kentucky needed an educated citizenry if it were to grow and thrive in the increasingly competitive industrial economy of the era. The commonwealth had a pair of venerable public universities in Louisville and Lexington, but the rural hinterland was largely underserved in higher education opportunities well into the years after World War I. The Purchase Area, for example, had just a normal school in Calloway County along with two small private religious colleges in Hickman County, Clinton College and Marvin College (later the Marvin University School), but they folded in 1913, 1915, and 1922, respectively, forcing college-bound students from the region to move far from home to pursue their degrees or forgo a postsecondary education.

Big changes were coming, though, when the Educational Commission of the General Assembly declared in the fall of 1921 that Kentucky needed "more and better teacher-training schools." Normal schools had first appeared in the 1830s to familiarize future educators with modern teaching standards, or "norms." Many evolved into teachers' colleges, then into major public universities over time. (Along with Murray State, Eastern Kentucky, Kentucky State, Morehead State, and Western Kentucky Universities all went through this process.) Before normal schools, most teachers had only a high school education and taught a narrow range of subjects, grammar especially, to a wide age range of students over academic years that were measured in weeks rather than months. Even decades after the first normal schools opened their doors, there were still only a handful in the state. By the turn of the century, however, Kentuckians demanded new normal schools that would boost the number of well-trained teachers, which would in turn prepare better-educated graduates for specialized college degrees.

In late 1921, the General Assembly began considering two new sites in the far eastern and western corners of Kentucky after having awarded the previous round of normal schools to Richmond (Eastern Kentucky State Normal School No. 1, forerunner to EKU) and Bowling Green (Western Kentucky State Normal School, forerunner to WKU) in 1906. These two normal schools created plenty of new educational opportunities beyond Louisville and Lexington, but they were still distant from potential students in the further reaches of the state during this age of poor roads and primitive automobiles. The Purchase Area in particular was almost an island cut off from the rest of Kentucky by the Tennessee River until Eggner Ferry Bridge connected Trigg and Marshall Counties in 1932.

The state was going to give far western Kentucky its first permanent normal school, but the question of where exactly to locate it remained to be seen. Community leaders from Benton, Hopkinsville, Mayfield, Murray, Paducah, Princeton, and other communities went to work preparing their bids, fiercely lobbying the commission on behalf of their respective towns. All of these competitors saw securing the normal school as a transformative opportunity to boost civic pride, provide exciting new opportunities for their people, and bring in a major engine for prosperity.

Rainey T. Wells outhustled his rivals to win this battle decisively for the people of Murray and Calloway County, who provided "loyal, continuous and unanimous support" during his pursuit of a normal school. Wells set Murray apart by raising an eye-watering $117,000 in cash (about $1.8 million in today's money) from 1,352 individual community donors. Some gave as little as $1, some as much as a few thousand. This seed money bought a large parcel of land on the undeveloped west side of town for a future campus and would cover the construction of its first building, sparing the state a costly outlay to begin operations if it chose Murray. Additionally, 350 local families pledged to offer fully furnished rooms in their welcoming homes for up to 2,000 student boarders, a generous offer that would allow instruction to begin immediately, before new dorms had been built. This tremendous outpouring of community support made the Educational Commission's decision easy; on September 17, 1922, it voted to grant Murray the new western Kentucky normal school.

There was one minor complication, though: the first classes at the newly established Murray State Normal School were scheduled for September 1923, before any actual campus buildings had

| Calloway County officials on the courthouse steps, 1922. |

been constructed. Wells had foreseen this and secured permission from the Murray Independent School District to temporarily operate out of the auditorium and several second floor classrooms in its brand new high school on 8th and Main Streets. The first cohort of eighty-seven student pioneers at this school-within-a-school did their studying in a makeshift reading room set up on the auditorium stage, working with a library book collection that was small enough to fit in an adjacent storage room. All of them lived in Murray, paying as much as $6 per week for room and board.

In September 1924, Murray State Normal School proudly opened the doors of the Administration Building (now Wrather West Kentucky Museum), an all-purpose space with classrooms, offices, science labs, a gymnasium, an auditorium, and, before the year was out, a cafeteria in the basement. As Wells's physical vision for the new school began to take shape, Murray State's first president, Dr. John Wesley Carr, imparted the nurturing culture and values for which it became widely known.

There was tremendous progress over the first fifteen years of this once modest little normal school. In 1926, it became Murray State Normal School and Teachers College to reflect the addition of new four-year degree programs, then in 1930 it was again renamed Murray State Teach-

| Murray branch of the First National Bank, 1920s. |

ers College, with another slate of offerings. The one-building campus of 1924 grew and expanded, first with the utilitarian Classroom Building (soon renamed the Liberal Arts Building and eventually Wilson Hall) and Wells Hall, originally a women's dormitory. Then it added two grandiose landmarks that signaled ambitions for a bigger and better future: the 3,000-seat Auditorium on the quad, now known as Lovett Auditorium, and the three-story Renaissance Revival-style Library on 15th Street, now Pogue Library. Student life was vibrant, music and theatre offered creative outlets, talented professors joined the faculty, and both men's and women's athletics programs enjoyed great success. Murray State was off to a very auspicious beginning.

Winning the bid for a normal school took real salesmanship, aggressive fundraising, and a keen political acumen. The commission was looking for a site with good road and rail links, clean water, and adequate medical facilities, as well as a general grab bag of other qualities it thought augured well for success. Wells submitted these photos to the Educational Commission to demonstrate that Murray indeed had all the infrastructure—a bank, a hotel, wide paved roads, and the backing of elected officials—to support a normal school.

Dr. Wells (1875–1958) served his community in many different ways during a long and distinguished career in public life, but this Calloway County native is revered most of all for the pivotal

The New Murray Hotel, 1920s.

role he played in establishing Murray State. Born just outside Murray on Christmas Day in 1875, Wells graduated with a B.A., an LL.B., and an M.A. from Southern Normal College in Huntingdon, Tennessee, then came back home to establish the Calloway Normal School in Kirksey at just twenty-four years old in 1899. He taught there for several years, then began practicing law in 1901. He married Tennie Daniel in 1896 and they had three children. Wells was elected to the state legislature in 1902 and later served as the state tax commissioner, a powerful position that allowed him to establish a strong political base throughout the commonwealth. As a politician, Wells championed better state funding for education across Kentucky, but without him at the helm Calloway's first normal school closed its doors in 1913. When the opportunity arose to locate another one in our region in 1921, he was determined to build it on a lasting foundation.

After the bid had been won, Wells continued to shape the new college right down to the campus blueprints. A fanatical basketball fan, he even came up with the Thoroughbred nickname for Murray State athletics teams. Wells served as Murray State's second president from 1926 to 1932 and presided over its first great building boom before handing the reins back to his trusted partner, Dr. John W. Carr. With the college running smoothly and a fresh LL.D. he had completed at the University of Kentucky (UK) in 1927, Dr. Wells returned his focus to the law. In 1933 he relocated to Omaha to become the general counsel of Woodmen of the World, a major insurance pro-

Dr. Rainey T. Wells, Kentucky legislator, founder, and second president of Murray State Normal School.

Dr. John W. Carr, first president of Murray State Normal School.

vider, and later won a case in front of the US Supreme Court. After retiring from the law in 1947, Dr. Wells returned to Murray, where he spent the last decade of his life in a newly built home and remained involved with the college he had created through sheer determination and great political skill.

The normal school's first president, Dr. John Wesley Carr (1859–1960), was a beloved Indiana transplant who earned the nickname "The Grand Old Man of Murray State College." Dr. Carr was very much a master teacher by the time he arrived in Murray, having accumulated decades of experience in various classroom roles, from a country school teacher to high school principal. At fifty-three years old in 1913, he completed a Ph.D. at New York University, then moved between several high-profile administrative positions before settling in as the Kentucky high school supervisor. Dr. Carr's credentials were impeccable, but Rainey T. Wells expected the state to name him Murray State's first president in recognition of his work to establish the college, and he was bitterly disappointed at being passed over for the position. Nevertheless, they worked together, developed a mutual respect, and ultimately became good friends. Dr. Carr understood how important it was to Wells to become president, so he gave up the position in 1926 to serve instead as dean.

Early sketch of the normal school campus from the architects at Joseph and Joseph.

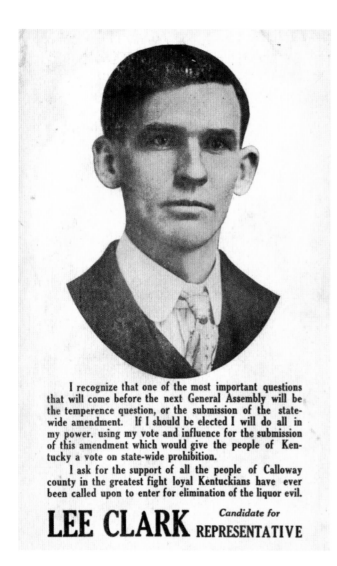

I recognize that one of the most important questions that will come before the next General Assembly will be the temperence question, or the submission of the state-wide amendment. If I should be elected I will do all in my power, using my vote and influence for the submission of this amendment which would give the people of Kentucky a vote on state-wide prohibition.

I ask for the support of all the people of Calloway county in the greatest fight loyal Kentuckians have ever been called upon to enter for elimination of the liquor evil.

LEE CLARK *Candidate for* REPRESENTATIVE

Representative Lee Clark, Kentucky legislator and longtime Murray State Normal School employee.

Dr. Carr was responsible for virtually every operational detail at the normal school in its early years, including hiring the first faculty and staff members, planning the first campus buildings with Wells, securing classroom space, advertising for students, arranging accommodations, budgeting, scheduling, setting rules and regulations, and, most importantly, designing curriculum. Building a school from scratch was challenging work, but Dr. Carr was up to the task. During two terms as president and two as dean before his retirement in 1940, he gained a reputation for his "patience, homely sense of humor, deliberativeness, loyalty to his associates, and love of freedom."

In the early 1920s, the future campus of Murray State was mostly undeveloped woodlot, a blank canvas for any number of design possibilities. Joseph and Joseph, a relatively new Louisville architectural firm that had gained renown for its work on the Kentucky State Fair building, won the contract to lay out a blueprint for the first campus building in May of 1923. Joseph and Joseph envisioned the future quad flanked on three sides by a horseshoe pattern of brand new buildings in an early visual aid that showed how its original construction project could fit into a campus master plan.

Murray State's iconic shield logo is an homage to the Scottish heraldic coat of arms of the family of John L. Murray (1806–42), a lawyer and Democrat who served the district first in the Kentucky House of Representatives from 1830 to 1835 and then in the US Congress from 1837 to 1839. Murray became the posthumous namesake of the new Calloway County seat chartered in October of 1843. The three stars in the escutcheon symbolize hope, endeavor, and achievement.

One of Rainey T. Wells's closest allies during the normal school bidding process was State Representative Lee Clark (1883–1960), a prominent farmer and businessman from nearby Lynn Grove. From the legislature, Clark "had militantly crusaded to lift farm life above the level of bare existence" and fought hard for better roads in western Kentucky. Clark had won the deep respect of his constituents and was mooted as a candidate for a US congressional seat, but he chose instead to serve the community closer to home. Clark worked for the college as the superintendent of build-

The three-star Murray shield at the entrance to Wilson Hall, one of many on campus.

ings and then later as manager of the college bookstore. His many decades of service to Murray State were first recognized with the dedication of a new men's dormitory, Clark Hall, in 1962. He was given a second great honor when Lee Clark College was created as part of the introduction of the residential college system in 1996.

The distinction of Murray State's first faculty hire went to E. H. Smith (mathematics), the principal of the Wingo school system in neighboring Graves County. He was part of the original 1923 teaching team of eight that included Belle Walker (science), Mary W. Moss (English), Irby Koffman (education, English, and athletics), Stella Pennington (music and art), James H. Hutchinson (education), William Caudill (history and geography), and Garland Murphey (art).

The second year of classes at Murray State began in September of 1924 in a brand new home, the Administration Building. This all-purpose building was explicitly designed to do a little bit of everything in the early years of campus expansion. Between a spacious auditorium, classrooms, and science labs, it had room for up to 500 students and could accommodate activities ranging from theatre productions and pep rallies to chapel services. It also had space for administrative offices, a post office, a gymnasium, and a cafeteria. At first the building had no equipment, furniture, books, or school materials, but President Carr and Rainey T. Wells secured backing from the state and the local high school to furnish and supply the building. In 1967 it was renamed for Marvin "M. O." Wrather, a long-serving and dedicated university administrator, and it was placed on the National Register of Historic Places in 1975. It has been home to the Wrather West Kentucky Museum since 1982.

E. H. SMITH, B. S.,
Directory Extension

Murray State has operated under the supervision of a board of regents appointed by the governor since its founding. The board dele-

E. H. Smith, professor of mathematics.

Administration Building, 1923, now the Wrather West Kentucky Museum.

gates administrative authority to the president in most aspects of daily business, but works with him or her to set strategic goals, to decide on major changes to degree programs, and to approve budgets, among many other important matters. The board began with five members and has since grown to eleven today, including regents representing faculty, staff, and students.

A terrible tragedy struck on November 27, 1924, Thanksgiving Day, while Murray State Normal School was playing a home game against West Tennessee Normal School of Memphis. In the first quarter, twenty-one-year-old varsity quarterback and Murray native Gilbert Graves was calling plays from the line. On his final touch, Graves wound up at the bottom of a pileup, badly injured. His

Murray State Normal School's first board members with President Carr: Laurine Wells Lovett, Tom Stokes, Prentice Thomas, and James Wilson (left to right). Absent is Dr. McHenry Rhoads, state superintendent of public instruction and first board chair.

father, Dr. Wildy H. Graves, rushed onto the field and took him to the hospital. Surgeons declared his neck had been broken and that he was paralyzed from the chin down. Graves died from his injuries on December 5, a little over a week later.

Graves had played football at Murray High before signing up for the first Murray State team. He was known by friends and relatives for his "noble nature, goodness of character and sunny smile" and was often referred to as the "Man of Murray." The inaugural 1925 edition of Murray State's yearbook, *The Shield,* was dedicated in his honor. As plans for a grand new home for Murray State football were unfolding decades later, the university's board of regents approved a motion in 1969 to name the thoroughfare around the future Roy Stewart Stadium "Gilbert Graves Drive" and install a plaque in Graves's honor near its front entrance. In true Murray State fashion, the memorial plaque was funded by the Alumni Association and community donors. The official dedication came on October 18, 1974, with Graves's sisters, Margaret Graves and Mildred Graves Hagan, present to mark the occasion.

Gilbert Graves, quarterback at Murray State Normal School.

Murray State's first cohort of students began organizing clubs and societies almost immediately after classes began. The Allenian Society, also known as A.C.E. (Aim, Conquer, Excel), was dedicated in honor of noted Kentucky author James Lane Allen as a vehicle for scholastic, artistic, and athletic pursuits. Along with it came the literary Wilsonian Society, named for former president and Nobel Peace Prize winner Woodrow Wilson. Next came a host of outlets for students pursuing interests in music, politics, English, and theatre. In 1926, female students created the Women's Self-Government Association to promote their interests and boost school spirit.

Once Murray State had graduated its first students, it needed an alumni association to help them keep them in touch with each other and their alma mater as they embarked on new teaching careers. This cohort wrapped up its graduation ceremony in the Little Chapel in the Administration Building on June 1, 1926, then immediately sat down to organize the Murray State Normal School and Teachers College Alumni Association. The new graduates elected Emma J. Helm as their first president. Helm stayed on campus as a sixth-grade teacher at the Training School from 1924 to 1941.

The first student-produced weekly newspaper, *The College News,* began publication on June 24, 1927. Its general tone was that of a serious broadsheet, but the editor could not resist the temptation to note in a front-page story that after having seen construction of the Murray State Auditorium firsthand, a visiting congressman from Georgia, W. D. Upshaw, vowed that "when I get back to Atlanta, I am going to shame the people of the city in their refusal to build an auditorium for Georgia Tech, and I shall point to the Murray State Teachers College's new auditorium to show what Kentucky is doing for her schools." In 1966, the paper was rebranded *The Murray State News* as the college evolved into a university. Still going strong almost a century later, it won the General Ex-

Allenian Society members, 1925.

Wilsonian Society members, 1926.

Gondee Tapp's 1926 scrapbook captures a full snapshot of 1920s student life with photos of friends, train receipts, candy advertisements, and a $1.50 basketball season ticket.

Students registering for classes in Wilson Hall, late 1920s.

Students of the first senior class at Murray State Normal School and Teachers College, 1926.

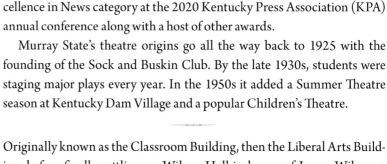

THE COLLEGE NEWS

OFFICIAL PUBLICATION MURRAY STATE TEACHERS COLLEGE, MURRAY, KENTUCKY

College News, Students,
Alumni, All For
M. S. T. C.

VOLUME ONE   MURRAY, KENTUCKY, FRIDAY, JULY 8, 1927.   NUMBER TWO.

BOARD APPROVE CERTIFICATES OF 160 STUDENTS

Hall Is Better
Young Student Has Chance Against Poison

FIRST SUMMER TERM TO BE AT END SATURDAY

Chapel Programs
Week's Presentations Are Among Season's Best

SCHULTZ GIVES FOURTH OF JULY ADDRESS HERE

New Band Head
Ewing Moore Fills Place Made Vacant by Lehnhoff

The College News, one of the first issues, July 8, 1927.

The Shield yearbook's first student staff members, 1925. The full collection of 1925 to 2008 editions can be found online at https://digitalcommons. murraystate.edu/yearbooks/.

cellence in News category at the 2020 Kentucky Press Association (KPA) annual conference along with a host of other awards.

Murray State's theatre origins go all the way back to 1925 with the founding of the Sock and Buskin Club. By the late 1930s, students were staging major plays every year. In the 1950s it added a Summer Theatre season at Kentucky Dam Village and a popular Children's Theatre.

Originally known as the Classroom Building, then the Liberal Arts Building, before finally settling on Wilson Hall in honor of James Wilson, a founding era member of the board of regents, Murray State's second building did something of everything in the early years of the normal school, just like the Administration Building next door. The library was on the third floor, and every subject from agriculture to science was taught in its classrooms at one point. The north central section of the ground floor held a gymnasium, the first campus home of Murray State basketball. The *Murray State News* has long operated out of Wilson Hall, and the campus radio station, WKMS, made its first broadcast there.

Below: Sock and Buskin members in a scene from *The Youngest*, 1927.

Right: Theatre advertisement for *Arsenic and Old Lace*, presented by Sock and Buskin members.

In 1918, construction was completed
on a stately two-story southern colonial
home that Rainey T. Wells built for his
family on a wooded thirty-two-acre par-
cel on the western end of town. Wells
named his home Edgewood in the quaint
English tradition. A few years later he
turned over most of his land to the new
normal school he had founded, but he
retained three acres around the home,
which was his primary residence during
the college's first decade. Two of his
children were married on the grounds,

NEW ADMINISTRATION AND CLASS ROOM BUILDING
MURRAY STATE NORMAL SCHOOL, MURRAY, KY.

and then two of his grandchildren were born in Edgewood. After Dr. Wells's business took him to
Omaha, he sold the property to Murray State in 1936 and it was renamed Oakhurst. It has since
been the campus home of nearly all of our presidents. When Dr. Wells retired and returned to Murray in 1946, he reclaimed the name Edgewood for his new home on South 12th Street.

"Edgewood," 1920s, home of Dr. Rainey T. Wells and family.

"Edgewood,"
Residence of Rainey T. Wells
Murray, Ky.

Dr. Clifton S. Lowry, 1948, professor of social sciences.

Caldwell County native Clifton "C. S." Lowry (1899–1992) joined the faculty to teach history and political science in 1925, terrorizing generations of Murray State students for forty-three years until his retirement as head of the Department of Social Sciences in 1968. Dr. Lowry was known as a provocative, often foul-mouthed instructor and a notoriously hard marker who demanded the very best from his students. Dr. Forrest C. Pogue, one of Murray State's most accomplished alumni to pursue an academic career of his own, credited Dr. Lowry for pushing him to the highest standards as an historian. The Lowry Library Annex was named in tribute to this legendary professor in 1967.

Most normal schools sent their students out to work alongside a teacher at the local public (also known as "common") school, but Murray State went a step further by creating its own training school operating out of Murray High in the summer of 1924. At first, it offered instruction for grades 1 through 8. Local parents were intrigued by the possibilities of the new venture, and 111 students enrolled for the first experimental summer session, which was so successful that the project continued into the regular academic year.

The Training School Institute moved to campus in the fall of 1924, with classes held in the Administration Building and Wilson Hall over the next three years. In 1928, construction on a new, dedicated Training School was completed, creating an on-campus venue that gave aspiring teachers practical experience in a controlled, real-world environment. Here, Murray State students were

The first campus dormitory, Wells Hall, opened in the fall semester in 1925. Originally designed to house up to 316 female students, it later added a cafeteria and an infirmary.

Costumed Training School students, 1920s.

Training School students in American colonial garb, 1926.

given an opportunity to teach a group of children under the supervision of faculty members, known as "critic teachers," who guided western Kentucky's best young educators.

In later years, the Training School came to be known as the Laboratory School and then the University School. Faculty members in particular were delighted to place their children in a modern, stand-alone school just steps away from their campus offices. The training school gained a reputation for turning out generations of high achievers, and its alumni remember their experiences fondly. In 1973, the training school closed and its remaining students transferred into the Murray Independent and Calloway County School Districts.

The annual May Day celebration on the campus quad was one of the biggest and most anticipated events on the college social calendar in Murray State's early years. This tradition had its origins in the ancient Roman spring celebration, the Floralia, which was imported to Britain and merged with a local Celtic holiday, Beltane. For centuries, Europeans celebrated May Day by decorating their villages with maypoles bedecked with flowers and streamers, then holding games and dances before

| May Day, 1931, with Lovett Auditorium and the Library in the background. |

anointing a May Queen. With industrialization in the late nineteenth century, May Day came to be associated around the world as a day of working-class activism, leading many American elites to worry over its new, seemingly radical direction. In 1894, President Grover Cleveland tried to undermine May Day by creating a distinctly American Labor Day holiday in early September, but it persisted nonetheless into the early Cold War years, when the Red Scare finally put it to bed for good as a mainstream public celebration.

In the summer of 1927, Murray State hired L. J. Hortin (1904–92), a junior reporter from the *St. Louis Post-Dispatch,* to teach a journalism course while he was on vacation. The arrangement worked out so well that he resigned from the paper and joined the faculty on a full-time basis, taking on all of the college's journalism courses, coaching the debate team, and supervising *The College News.* Hortin, a widely popular professor known to his students as "the Chief," left Murray State in 1947 to become head of the Department of Journalism at Ohio University, but he returned to Mur-

| Training School students at May Day celebration, 1920s. |

Murray State's first registrar and the namesake of Hester Hall, Cleo Gillis Hester (1890–1980), assigned a growing student body to the right classes from 1927 to 1960.

ray State University in 1967 when an opportunity to build a full journalism program with graduate offerings opened up at his first academic home. He was an inaugural inductee to the Kentucky Journalism Hall of Fame in 1981.

Every year since 1980, the Student Government Association has handed the prestigious Max Carman Outstanding Teacher Award to the most effective and inspiring instructor on campus. The award is named for Dr. Max Carman, a beloved math professor who taught at Murray State from 1928–1974 and holds the distinction of being one of the longest serving faculty members.

Walter Blackburn (1908–74) joined the faculty at Murray State in 1930 as a chemistry professor and completed his Ph.D. at the University of Illinois in 1944. He specialized in synthetic rubber and consulted with the DuPont Chemical Company on production of this vital wartime commodity. After many years as head of the chemistry department, Dr. Blackburn became dean of the School of Arts and Sciences in 1968. The university named Blackburn Science Building in honor of this outstanding instructor and administrator.

For over a half century, Murray and Calloway County residents have enjoyed exploring the 170,000-acre Land Between the Lakes National Recreation Area right in their backyard. Before mid-century dam projects upriver created Kentucky Lake and Lake Barkley, local residents had to travel farther

Left: Dr. L. J. Hortin, professor of journalism.

Center: Dr. Max Carman, professor of mathematics.

Right: Dr. Walter Blackburn, professor of chemistry.

Faculty, staff, and their families at a fish fry on Reelfoot Lake, 1930.

to find great park space. Seen here are Murray State Teachers College faculty and staff enjoying a fish fry in 1930 at Reelfoot Lake State Park in northwestern Tennessee.

The first three campus buildings in the mid-1920s all served essential functions for a fledgling teachers college, but the fourth was a grandiose symbol of Murray State's ambitions to grow. The 3,000-seat Auditorium on the campus quad, now known as Lovett Auditorium, was the largest college facility of its kind in Kentucky when it opened its doors in 1928. It was widely considered the finest

Interior of Lovett Auditorium, 1930s.

Library, now Pogue Library, at Murray State Teachers College, 1930s.

Students in the library reading room, 1940s.

auditorium in the region. The stage was used for community gatherings, speeches, theatre, and musical performances, but it was also built large enough to double as the home for the college basketball team until the Health Building (now John W. Carr Hall) was constructed in 1937. This gave the college a dual-purpose arts and entertainment venue that boosted its profile significantly throughout the region. Murray State later renamed the auditorium for Laurine Wells Lovett, a founding regent, daughter of Dr. and Mrs. Wells, and an accomplished pianist.

Murray State's library was well-traveled in the early years, migrating from its first spot in Murray High to the Administration Building, then the Liberal Arts Building, and then finally in 1931 to a spectacular purpose-built home at 15th and Olive Streets. The new four-story library building immediately became an iconic Murray landmark for the remarkable craftsmanship of its ornate columns and striking woodwork, but there was a minor political controversy over the cost of its "gold doors" on the front and quad side entrances. The doors were actually bronze, and while many at the time saw them as a Depression era extravagance, the originals still stand to this day. In a more serious nod to the era of its construction, the etching "the hope of democracy depends on the diffusion of knowledge" on the front face of the library was a fitting motto for the challenging decade ahead. With the addition of a new library in 1978, the building took on its current role as Pogue Special Collections Library, home to thousands of treasured and unique relics of west Kentucky history. The grand reading room is named in honor of Wells T. Lovett (1923–2013), an attorney, longtime regent, and the Oakhurst-born grandson of Rainey T. and Tennie Wells.

The first grand men's dorm on campus, the 38,000-square-foot Ordway Hall, opened in 1931 and served as home to thousands of Thoroughbreds until it was converted to office and academic

Ordway Hall, male dormitory, 1930s.

unit space in 1972. The university preserved its original facade just off the campus gates on the north side of Olive and 15th Streets when the building was razed in June 2013 to make way for a new green space next to Waterfield Library.

By 1932, Murray State had graduated enough classes that it could welcome alumni back every fall for a grand Homecoming. Seen here is the "Old-Fashioned Garden" float.

Murray State football enjoyed some of its greatest successes under Coach Roy Stewart (1901–80), who led the Thoroughbreds for twelve seasons, from 1932 to 1945. Stewart ended his football coaching career with a 60–33–11 record, highlighted by his undefeated 1933 squad (9–0) and the 1937 team that went 8–1–1. Both were Southern Intercollegiate Athletic Conference champions. Stewart was the college athletics director from 1941 until his retirement in 1966. He had a lasting legacy as one of the founders of the Ohio Valley Conference (OVC), created in 1948. The OVC originally included Western Kentucky University and the University of Louisville along with a cast of our well-known sporting rivals. Stewart earned an induction into the Murray State Hall of Fame in 1971 and then another in the OVC Hall of Fame in 1977 for his efforts. His looming influence on Murray State football is still evident today; when the university opened its current facility in 1973, a multi-million-dollar 16,800-seater, it made perfect sense to name it Roy Stewart Stadium.

Coach Roy Stewart, athletics director.

The 1933 football team seen here was one of the most dominant in Murray State history. Its crushing defense shut out the opposition in five of its nine games, while the offense ran up the score in a 70–7 home victory over Middle Tennessee, then humiliated the Louisville Cardinals 54–6 on the road. The Rose Bowl was the country's only college football

Football players from the 1933 team.

| A football game at Carlisle Cutchin Stadium, 1934. |

bowl game in 1933, so one can only speculate how this Roy Stewart super team would have fared under the national spotlight.

Murray State football was the first addition to the athletics program in the fall of 1923, with home games played at the Murray High Field. After the migration to campus the following year, the college built a temporary field on the future site of the Fine Arts Building. Carlisle Cutchin, who had previously coached at Mayfield High School, led the Thoroughbreds to an impressive 37–11–4 record from 1925 to 1930 while pulling triple duty as coach for the basketball and baseball teams. In 1934, Murray State honored him with the opening of the brand new 6,000-seat Carlisle Cutchin Stadium between Chestnut and Payne Streets. Cutchin Field was home to Thoroughbred football for almost forty years and now hosts home matches for the highly successful Racer women's soccer team.

| Coach Carrie Allison (later White) (far right) with the Lady Thoroughbreds basketball team, 1929. |

The first Murray State women's basketball game was played all the way back on January 18, 1929. While the Lady Thoroughbreds lost that first contest to Union University, they did go on to host and win the Mississippi Valley Conference tournament later that season. The team secured an invitation to compete in the eight-team Amateur Athletic Union national tournament, but declined because Coach Carrie Allison had fallen ill. The women's basketball program appears to have folded in 1935, possibly due to a lack of funds or a dearth of suitable regional competitors during the Great Depression, but it was resurrected in 1971 as women's college sports expanded all across the country.

One of Murray State's first star athletes was Dew Drop Rowlett, née Brumley (1911–93), who was unguardable on the court from 1933 to 1935 and once put up 62 points in a single game. Rowlett, a native of northeastern Mississippi, was recruited by Roy Stewart out of Freed-Hardeman College in Tennessee after dominant performances in the 1931 and 1932 Mississippi Valley Conference tournaments. The winning pitch that got her to transfer to Murray State from her junior college was the offer of a basketball scholarship in exchange for sweeping corridors and waiting on male athletes in the Wells Hall dining room. After graduation, she played semipro basketball for the Tupelo

Dew Drop Brumley, Lady Thoroughbred, 1930s.

Red Wings and was named an Amateur Athletic Union All-American. A lifelong educator, she came back to Murray State in 1965 as a professor of health, physical education, and recreation. After the women's basketball program was reinstated, she served as its head coach from 1971 until 1978, leading the team to four regional tournaments and four runner-up finishes in Association for Intercollegiate Athletics for Women district tournaments. Rowlett was inducted into the Murray State Hall of Fame in 1993.

The quad, view from the roof of the Liberal Arts Building, 1930s.

| The Hut restaurant at 15th and Olive Streets, 1930s. |

Boldly advertising "everything good to eat," The Hut opened its doors in 1931 on the corner of 15th and Olive Streets, becoming the first off-campus hangout spot for Murray State students. Owners Eugene and Ruth Hughes suffered a great tragedy when their business burned down in 1945, but they rebuilt The Hut with an additional wing in the summer of 1946. In October 1952, the Hughes family sold The Hut to former employee Jack Ward and his wife, Millie, and they in turn ran this popular local business until it closed in August 1973.

| *Right, top:* Students dressed to their Roaring Twenties best at a soiree in the Liberal Arts Building. |

| *Right, bottom:* Another student dance, third floor of the Library, 1930s. |

| 2 |

Surviving Hard Times

1936–1948

Introduction

AFTER AN INAUGURAL DECADE OF GROWTH, MURRAY STATE'S administrators faced unimaginable difficulties as the nation plunged into economic collapse in the 1930s and then war in the 1940s. Kentucky was suffering badly from end to end; coal country grew desperate when demand collapsed as factories closed, unemployment was rampant in the cities, those who retained their jobs saw their wages cut dramatically, prices for agricultural commodities fell to record lows, and children across the state often went to bed hungry at night. There was limited respite on the farms of western Kentucky, where a family could at least produce its own food, but for years on end it seemed as though the entire American system was on the brink of collapse. There was no way for Murray State to insulate itself from the nation's hardships, which hit campus as enrollment dropped precipitously, revenues fell off, and the college was left struggling to pay its bills.

The community as a whole, however, showed tremendous resilience and the highly adept second generation of college leadership rose to the challenge during these dark days. Rainey T. Wells had artfully managed his political connections in Frankfort to found the normal school in the early 1920s. At this juncture the new college president, Dr. James

Richmond, repeatedly tapped into his close relationship with the Roosevelt administration in Washington to prevent Murray State from becoming a casualty of economic depression and war.

Dr. Richmond was much more than a regional party boss. He had run two successful state-wide presidential campaigns for Franklin Roosevelt, earning trust and respect from the most powerful man in the world. Dr. Richmond was such an esteemed educator that Congress called on him to lead a hearing in 1934 to discuss emergency federal relief. His efforts helped free up $17 million in urgently needed appropriations to keep schools going across thirty states. Two years later, the White House summoned him back to Washington for a personal meeting with the president on how best to utilize a second round of federal aid to American schools. As college president, Dr. Richmond fostered close ties between Murray State and the Roosevelt administration, repeatedly securing the relief the college needed to continue operations. Just prior to Richmond's arrival, the federal government's major infrastructure-building body, the Works Progress Administration, had built Carlisle Cutchin Stadium for Murray State as part of a job creation effort. Later in 1938, Dr. Richmond lobbied the National Youth Administration (NYA) to begin a resident work project on campus, bringing in subsidies for fifty new students to learn a vocation and gain practical skills at Murray State. NYA students also doubled as campus construction workers, erecting a new dorm, a wall, and part of the Fine Arts Building.

Dr. Richmond had mostly stabilized Murray State's Depression-related financial concerns, but America's entry into World War II in December 1941 created a much more acute set of problems. Enrollment was stable at a healthy 1,100 in 1940, but it cratered to just 289 by 1943–1944 as male students left en masse to join the military. Without a very dramatic and immediate solution to this student shortage, Murray State would have had to shutter its doors, possibly for good.

As it turned out, the college had made a very shrewd investment as war clouds were looming in October 1940 when it inaugurated its Civilian Pilot Training Program at a small airfield four miles south of Murray. This was a relatively small-scale affair with only twenty students at any given time, but the program had solid instructors and a ground school component that taught essential subjects, such as civil aeronautics regulations, construction and repair, meteorology, navigation, parachutes, radio, and safety devices. This meant that when the US Navy came looking for sites to train future pilots in 1942, Dr. Richmond was able to pitch more than just Murray State's ties with the Roosevelt administration. The college already had all of the physical and human infrastructure the navy needed to accommodate hundreds of cadets—classrooms, dorms, and civilian science and math instructors—and was immediately ready to contribute to the war effort. This is ultimately why the navy set up operations in Murray, a town tucked away in a landlocked state nearly 500 miles from the nearest body of salt water.

Some of Murray State's most remarkable alumni came through campus during these lean years. This cohort of military veterans included the US Navy's first female pilot, Anna Mayrell Johnson, and the combat historian for the Second Army, Dr. Forrest C. Pogue. On the stage, there was actor Hal Riddle, who survived a brush with death while serving in the Pacific Theater in the navy. On the gridiron, there was fighter pilot Claude "Mac" McRaven, a multisport star who was the first Murray State graduate to play in a Big Four professional sport, and army veteran Pete Gudauskas, who played for the 1943 NFL champion Chicago Bears. Joe Fulks, one of the greatest ever Murray State basketball players, saw hell on earth with the Marine Corps during its island hopping campaign in the Pacific Ocean. Future business and agriculture leader Bill Garrett, a tank gunnery officer, crossed the bridge at Remagen in March 1945, busting open Germany's western defenses and helping Allied forces bring the war to an end in Europe. Many others served bravely, and too many of them made the ultimate sacrifice.

Americans could begin imagining what life would be like once peace returned after the successful D-Day landings in early June of 1944. The Roosevelt administration steered the Servicemen's Readjustment Act of 1944, better known as the G.I. Bill, through Congress later that month to help ease the veteran transition back to civilian life. Among its many generous provisions was grant money for vocational training and higher education. After having survived the Depression and the war, Dr. Richmond's last act was to ensure that Murray State offered a warm welcome for homecoming veterans who had given so much for the freedom of the world. To this end, the college took measures that benefitted all students, such as restoring many prewar courses and establishing new programs, including industrial arts, military science, nursing, and communications, along with targeted innovations, including veteran-specific programs and housing along with reduced tuition.

| Dr. James Richmond, the third president. |

Like Dr. Carr before him, Murray State's third president, James Howell Richmond (1884–1945), came to the college directly from a high-ranking position with the state government. Richmond was born in the village of Ewing, Virginia, near the mouth of the Cumberland Gap and went on to study at Lincoln Memorial University in nearby Harrogate before completing his bachelor's degree at the University of Tennessee in 1907. After graduation, he was a well-traveled classroom teacher who made stops in Tennessee, Kentucky, and Texas before settling in as a high school principal in Louisville in 1914. From 1928 to 1936, he was first the high school supervisor and then the superintendent of public instruction for the Kentucky State Department of Education.

A staunch and well-connected Democrat, Dr. Richmond assumed the college presidency in 1936 in the midst of a long national economic crisis and faced unimaginable pressure as revenues and enrollment nearly collapsed. It has often been said that Rainey T. Wells and John Carr built Murray State, but Dr. Richmond saved it from probable ruin by securing the V-12 Naval Pre-Flight Preparatory Training Unit in 1942. Through the war years Dr. Richmond gave weekly chapel services on campus, encouraging students to focus on their studies as a patriotic duty right up to the moment they were called on to join the military. The war years were stressful for everyone on campus, but perhaps Dr. Richmond most of all. He was the first and only Murray State president to die in office. He died on July 24, 1945, a little over a month before the end of the war.

Murray State's first purpose-built athletics home was the Health Building, which opened in 1937 with three gymnasiums, boxing and wrestling rings, a weight room, a pool, and classrooms. In its early years it served primarily as the home of the physical education and nursing programs. Over the years it has been renamed the Carr Health Building and most recently John W. Carr Hall.

Murray State men's basketball began play in 1925, and the program has become the undeniable pride of campus. With an all-time mark of 1,709 wins and 919 losses as of the end of the 2021–2022 season, Murray

The first campus pool, Health Building, 1930.

State is one of the winningest college basketball programs in the country, ahead of perennial powerhouses such as Notre Dame, Connecticut, and Marquette. The team's first home was the Classroom/Liberal Arts Building gym, then it played for a decade on the stage of Lovett Auditorium, and finally in 1937 it got a proper court in the Health Building's North Gym. Over three seasons from 1935 to 1938, Carlisle Cutchin's dominant teams put up a cumulative record of 72 wins and 9 losses, marking Murray State as a highly desirable college for potential recruits throughout the region. Seen here is a group shot of the 1936–1937 squad in Lovett Auditorium.

Claude "Mac" McRaven is seen with the 1936–1937 men's basketball team in the back row, second from left, beside Coach Carlisle Cutchin.

Future physician David Booker (foreground on the stool) working in the original chemistry lab in the basement of the Administration Building.

Campus Lights, an annual winter theatre production held at Lovett Auditorium, is the longest-running cultural tradition at Murray State. Students have been entirely responsible for all aspects of the production, from choreography to performing, while its format has evolved from variety shows to Broadway-style performances. Campus Lights was launched in 1938 by Phi Mu Alpha Sinfonia, a men's music fraternity, as a fundraiser to establish the Gamma Delta chapter on campus. Early productions were a great success, but the Japanese attack on Pearl Harbor in 1941 prompted many male students to join the war effort, leaving Campus Lights short of performers. The women of Sigma Alpha Iota valiantly stepped in to keep the tradition going, temporarily renaming the show "Campus Dim Out" to honor those who had left to fight for their country. At war's end, Sigma Alpha Iota and Phi Mu Alpha made Campus Lights a joint effort.

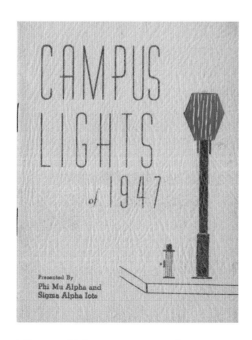

| Campus Lights program, 1947. |

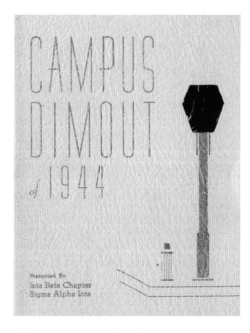

| Wartime Campus Dim Out program, 1944. |

Calloway County native Marvin "M. O." Wrather (1900–70) dedicated most of his adult life to Murray State after graduating with the first four-year class in 1926. Wrather began his career as a teacher, then rose to Calloway County school superintendent before his hiring at Murray State in 1938. He filled a number of important administrative roles over the years, including director of public relations, secretary of the Alumni Association, executive vice president, and acting president on three separate occasions. His daughter, Anne Wrather Hoke, recalled that "he just loved people, and especially young people. Seeing Murray State graduates excel thrilled him." Murray State renamed the original Administration Building as Wrather Hall in 1967, then it awarded him an honorary LL.D. in 1969 in recognition of his many decades of service.

Administrator M. O. Wrather, one of Murray State's first graduates.

When Price "Pop" Doyle (1896–1967) from Peru, Nebraska, joined the faculty as a professor of music in 1930, he brought enough passion to establish a thriving fine arts program that com-

Dr. Price Doyle leads the Murray State Orchestra at WSM Radio in Nashville in 1935.

Golden Era actor Hal Riddle.

Riddle's first film, *Onionhead*, 1958.

plemented Murray State's original educator-oriented offerings. He headed the Department of Fine Arts from its creation in 1939 until his retirement in 1957.

The theatre department at Murray State has nurtured the talents of generations of young actors, and a number of our alumni have gone on to enjoy great success in Hollywood, on Broadway, and on the small screen. The first was Hal Riddle (1919–2009), a 1942 graduate and World War II navy veteran who built up a great reputation as a character actor over his forty-year career in television and film. He generously willed his entire estate to Murray State, a gift that included hundreds of vintage movie posters and autographed memorabilia from Hollywood's biggest stars.

Pete Gudauskas (17) and the 1943 NFL champion Chicago Bears. Photo courtesy of the Chicago Bears.

| Nash House. |

| Dr. William Nash, dean. |

Pete "The Toe" Gudauskas (1916–2003) was one of the first Murray State student athletes to play professionally in a Big Four sport. Gudauskas was primarily a tackle for Murray State from 1937 to 1939, but his skills as a kicker opened up a professional opportunity on the gridiron. As was common of the era, Gudauskas's career was interrupted by military service, but he played in parts of four seasons in the NFL and was a member of the 1943 championship-winning Chicago Bears squad.

One of the most striking interwar homes standing in Murray today is Nash House on North 16th Street. It was originally the residence of Dr. William G. Nash (1899–1984), a longtime academic dean who served at Murray State from 1940 to 1970. Nash House has been home to the Murray State University Foundation since 1998. The foundation was established in 1946 and now manages roughly $180 million in donated assets.

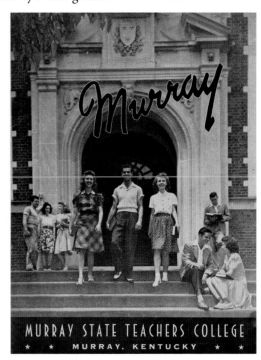

| For the happy coeds featured on the cover of the 1942 *College Bulletin*, some aspects of campus life proceeded as normal through the war years.

| *Above:* In formation, 1943. |

| *Left:* Uniformed navy cadets. |

Thanks to Dr. Richmond's efforts, Murray State was one of just 131 colleges across the country to secure a host site for a Naval Pre-Flight Preparatory Training Unit. This mutually beneficial arrangement gave the college an opportunity to do its part for the war effort while bringing in a major influx of cadets and $100,000 in federal aid. The training school was designed to produce officers for the US Navy and the Marine Corps over an eight-week course that included military drill, physical education, physics, mathematics, military discipline and courtesy, navigation, meteorology, servicing of aircraft, civil air regulations, radio code, and aircraft identification, in addition to thirty-five hours of actual flying. The first cohort of 250 navy cadets arrived on campus on January 6, 1943, and by the summer over 1,100 had enrolled for training courses.

The navy began closing its pre-flight training units in the fall of 1944 as the Second World War began to wind down. The last of the cadets departed when the Murray unit was officially closed on October 31, 1944, but a naval academic refresher course remained active on campus until December 15, 1945. Before the war, almost all Murray State students came from the immediate area, but after its conclusion many naval flight school alumni from further afield came back to enroll in civilian programs on the G.I. Bill.

| Dean of Women Anna Mayrell Johnson (right) and close friend Jane Haseldon. |

In 1908, a handful of pioneering women joined the US Navy Nurse Corps, and many more followed them into the military as office staff during the world wars. In these early days they were confined to clerical and nursing roles that conformed to accepted gender norms of the era. This changed in the summer of 1942 when President Roosevelt created a navy women's reserve program, Women Accepted for Volunteer Emergency Service (WAVES), that allowed women to enlist and serve as officers. Murray State's Anna Mayrell Johnson, an avid amateur pilot who co-owned a plane with her close friend Jane Haseldon, the dean of women at Transylvania University, seized this opportunity in 1943.

Johnson (1910–93) completed her M.S. at Murray State and an M.A. at UK, then came back to teach political science from 1932 to 1947. From 1935 to 1939 she was the dean of women, which made her one of the most important campus administrators. The onset of war brought fuel rationing and by extension an end to Johnson's recreational flights with Haseldon in the skies around Lexington. So, faced with a choice over whether to abandon her great passion or continue it in a military uniform, Johnson eagerly joined the WAVES program.

What makes Johnson so unique in American military history is that she joined the navy as a pilot, which had been exclusively male territory. Lieutenant Commander Johnson holds the distinction of being the first American woman in World War II to be issued flight orders. In the few surviving blurry, black and white photos of the war-era flight school at Murray State, Johnson is typically seen in her leather bomber jacket sporting a confident grin, the only woman in a sea of male instructors and cadets. She almost certainly would have been a ferocious combatant had she been deployed to an active theater overseas. After the war, Johnson earned a Ph.D. in international law from American University and continued to pursue her love of flight through the Ninety-Nines, a club for women pilots founded by Amelia Earhart. President Harry Truman abolished the WAVES program in 1948, and American women had to wait until the 1970s for the opportunity to train as naval pilots and officers, but Dr. Johnson and her cohort undoubtedly paved the way for their gains a generation later.

The Smith-Johnson Genealogy and History Room at Pogue Library was dedicated in 2019 to Lieutenant Commander Anna Mayrell Johnson, her sister and longtime Calloway County educator Mary Johnson Smith, and Mary's daughter Dr. Brinda Smith, who earned a bachelor's degree in physical education and library science from Murray State in 1954, an M.A. from Louisiana State University, and a Ph.D. from the University of Southern Mississippi. All three of these extraordinary women represent the very best of Murray State.

| Dr. Forrest C. Pogue, professor of history, 1937. |

Of all the talented faculty members at Murray State over the past century, one of the most remarkable academic careers belongs to Forrest Pogue (1912–94), a history professor whose journey took him from a west Kentucky family farm to the corridors of power in Washington via Murray State and the battlefields of Normandy. Pogue was born in Eddyville and grew up among storytellers at the dawn of the radio age. He graduated from Murray State Teachers College in 1931, then earned an M.A. at UK and a Ph.D. from Clark University. He came home to join the history faculty at Murray State in 1933 and taught at the college until he was drafted into the army in 1942.

Dr. Pogue completed basic training at Fort McClellan in Alabama and spent his first year at war as a private, carrying out a number of mundane tasks, such as digging trenches and filing paperwork. In the spring of 1943 he was assigned to Memphis for a role more fitting his academic background: combat historian for the US Second Army just as American and Allied forces were about to launch a campaign to liberate western Europe from Nazi occupation. Dr. Pogue was deployed to England in 1944, then France following the D-Day landings, and later Belgium during the crucial Battle of Bulge that winter. He spent eleven months interviewing wounded soldiers fresh from the battlefield, earning a Bronze Star and the French Croix de Guerre for his pioneering work in the field of military oral history.

On his discharge in October 1945, Dr. Pogue was hired by the army to continue his work as a civilian. General Dwight D. Eisenhower, who led the war effort in Europe, gave Dr. Pogue responsibility for writing the official history of Supreme Allied Command Europe. This gave Dr. Pogue the opportunity to meet and interview many top wartime leaders from the United States, Britain, France, and elsewhere. His work culminated in the publication of his first book, *United States Army in World War II: European Theater of Operations: The Supreme Command,* in 1954.

Dr. Pogue briefly returned to Murray State in 1954; then two years later he accepted the prestigious role of director of the George C. Marshall Research Foundation in Lexington, Virginia. In this new post he pored over 3.5 million documents over the course of three decades to write the definitive, four-volume biography of General Marshall. Known as "the organizer of war" as US Army chief of staff during World War II, Marshall later served in pivotal early Cold War roles as special envoy to China, secretary of defense, and secretary of state. Viking Press published the first volume in 1963 and the last in 1987, three years after Dr. Pogue had retired.

In his later years, Dr. Pogue served as director of the Eisenhower Institute for Historical Research, also teaching at George Washington University, the US Army War College, and the Virginia Military Institute. He served on a number of military history advisory boards and was the president of the Oral History Association, among other organizations. In 1978 Murray State dedicated its grandest campus building, the Pogue Special Collections Library, in honor of his career achievements. He spent his final years back home in Murray, where his great adventure began.

Many supremely talented basketball players have donned the blue and gold over the past century, and one of them, Joe Fulks, was immortalized with the ultimate honor of induction into the Naismith Memorial Basketball Hall of Fame. Fulks (1921–76), a slight, 6'5", 190-pound point guard known as the "Kuttawa Clipper" and "Jumpin' Joe," was the star of the excellent 1941 and 1942 Thoroughbred teams that put up a remarkable 39–9 record.

In May of 1943, Fulks left Murray State to join the Marine Corps just as it began a grinding campaign to liberate a string of Pacific islands from Japanese military occupation. He rose to the rank of corporal and saw action with the 3rd Battalion, 9th Marines, in the bloody American victories at Guam and Iwo Jima. Fulks joined the Marine Corps All-Star Leathernecks basketball team during the war, which gave him an opportunity to continue playing against high-level competition. After his discharge, he signed with the Philadelphia Warriors of the Basketball Association of America (BAA) for the 1946–1947 season. As a twenty-five-year-old rookie, he won the league scoring title with 23.2 points per game, seven points better than his nearest rival, for his championship-winning team. Fulks continued performing at a similar level for his next two seasons, and *The Sporting News*

Philadelphia Warriors star "Jumpin' Joe" Fulks.

declared him "the greatest basketball player in the country" in 1949. That year he put up one of his greatest highlights, a BAA-record 63-point game, a mark that stood for a decade.

After eight years with the Warriors, Fulks retired at age thirty-two after the 1953–1954 season. He was one of the greatest scorers of the BAA/early NBA-era, racking up 8,003 points over his professional career, earning three All-BAA First Team honors and two NBA All-Star selections. As the pioneer of the jump shot, he was undeniably one of the game's brightest stars, and this merited him a spot on the NBA's silver anniversary team in 1971, along with luminaries such as Bill Russell, Bob Cousy, and George Mikan.

Fulks returned home to Kuttawa after his playing days and worked for a time as a Kentucky-Tennessee scout for the Philadelphia 76ers. He traded his fame into jobs as a foreman at the GAF Corporation in Calvert City and later the Kentucky State Penitentiary in Eddyville, where he served as a recreation officer. In 1978 he was posthumously inducted into the Naismith Hall of Fame. Murray State retired his number 26.

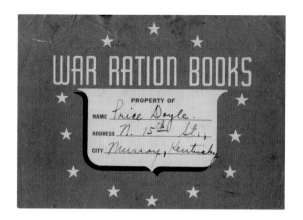

The war brought hardships on the home front as basic commodities Americans took for granted were in short supply. Seen here is Dr. Price Doyle's ration book.

By the time the fighting ended in September of 1945, fifty-one Murray State students had given their lives to liberate Europe and Asia from the fascist yoke. They are honored in this In Memoriam roster in Lovett Auditorium.

After Dr. Richmond's untimely death in 1945, the presidency passed to a fellow Virginian, Dr. Ralph Woods (1898–1973), who presided over a tentative period of stabilization immediately after the war, followed by nearly two decades of the most explosive growth in Murray State history. Woods served in the US Army during World War I and completed a bachelor of philosophy degree at Berea College in 1921 before starting his career as an educator as a teacher, then a principal at Ballard County High School from 1923 to 1926. He completed a B.S. in agriculture and an M.A. in education at UK in 1923 and 1927, respectively, and finally a Ph.D. from Cornell University in 1930. Dr. Woods mostly taught agricultural education at UK from 1928 to 1945, but from 1936 to 1945 he split his time between the university and a variety of state and federal educational initiatives.

With the Depression and war behind it, Murray State was primed for growth under an able leader. Dr. Woods was Murray State's longest serving president at twenty-three years on the job, and he made the very most of the opportunities created during America's extended postwar boom. Most notably, he oversaw Murray State Teachers College's transition to a full college in 1948 and then ultimately to a university in 1966. During his tenure a range of popular new departments were added (such as industrial arts, nursing, military science, and communications), enrollment exploded from under 600 to over 7,000, the faculty grew from just 62 to 376, Greek life took root and flourished, and dozens of new buildings went up across campus.

Dr. Hugh Oakley (1912–2000) joined the faculty in 1946 and was immediately tasked with creating a new Department of Industrial Arts with vocational offerings that would cater to demobilized veterans. His greatest challenge was finding a place to put it after his initial plans to house it in either the Science Building or the old Farm Shop proved unworkable. Dr. Oakley's heavy benches, woodworking equipment, and electrical labs were originally set up in the Administration

Building, then they migrated to Fine Arts, but neither of these temporary spaces had enough room to accommodate his vision. In 1947 he came up with a better solution in collaboration with the Federal Works Administration: dismantling three disused 50-foot by 110-foot war-era ordinance buildings in Illinois, packing them up, shipping them to Murray, and then rebuilding them on campus. This cost Murray State a bargain basement sum, but more importantly it allowed the college to offer a

President Ralph Woods (left) and Dr. Ray Mofield on WPAD radio.

fuller range of industrial arts courses in drafting, metalworking, woodworking, and electronics to eager veterans as quickly as possible. After its launch in the Industrial Arts Building, the program grew from just ninety-six students in its first year, 1946, to over 1,000 by 1969. The industrial arts program became the College of Industry and Technology in 1973, with Dr. Oakley serving as its dean until his retirement in 1977.

Dr. Hugh Oakley, professor of industrial arts.

Industrial Arts Building, 1947.

| 3 |

The Postwar Boom

1948–1966

Introduction

A GENERAL OPTIMISM PREVAILED ACROSS THE LAND ONCE THE extended privations of the Depression and the war years finally came to an end. As the postwar American economy boomed, mass unemployment became a thing of the past, wages swelled, and families grew. At an individual level, this gave both a generation of homecoming veterans and their offspring the means to pursue wide-ranging opportunities in higher education that would have been unthinkable just decades earlier. After coming through the greatest challenge it had ever faced during the war, Murray State rode the crest of this wave for a long, extended Golden Era.

A semblance of normalcy began to return to campus by the fall of 1946 as demobilized veterans resumed or began their studies. Their arrival was followed almost immediately by a period of tremendous growth. Enrollment swelled to over 7,000 by the end of the Woods era in 1968, and the number of faculty members nearly tripled to serve this new generation of students. New buildings sprouted in all directions like mushrooms—thirty-one were added to the ten standing at the outset of Dr. Woods's tenure—including many campus landmarks, such as the Harry Lee Waterfield Student Union Building. Murray State's mission had grown far beyond its roots as a teachers college with the addition of popular new programs, leading to a formal transition to a full college in 1948 by act of the state legislature. Murray State subsequently reorganized itself into five schools—Applied Sciences and Technology, Arts and Sciences, Business, Education, and the Graduate School—as a precursor to its final evolution into a university in 1966.

This was also a period of watershed cultural change at both the national and local levels. In 1950, the state government bowed to pressure by amending the Day Law, which had blocked access to public colleges and universities to Black students, granting institutions the power to decide admissions on the merits of individual applicants regardless of race. This move acknowledged that the Kentucky State College for Negroes in Frankfort did not have the resources to offer "separate but equal" graduate offerings and created the possibility of total desegregation in higher education across the state. This was a hugely significant development, but it was ultimately the US Supreme Court's landmark *Brown v. Board of Education* decision in 1954 that dramatically accelerated the timetable for the badly overdue integration of Kentucky's colleges and universities.

Murray State desegregated peacefully in the summer of 1955, before any of the other regional colleges in Kentucky, when Mary Ford Holland, an unassuming, middle-aged classroom teacher from Lyon County, transferred into the education program. That fall she was joined by a full slate of graduates from Murray's Frederick Douglass High School, made up of Geneva Arnold, Bobby Leonard Brandon, Arlene France Keys, and Willie Earl Perry. Still, the most visible symbol of this new opening came when Dennis Jackson, a hometown hero who transferred to Murray State in 1960, integrated our athletics department and ushered in a transformation of the entire OVC. One of Jackson's fondest memories from his playing days was directly tied to his role in bringing social change to the community. "I remember one day, my father came in from taking out the garbage. He had seen a group of white boys playing football across the yard. In celebration of a catch, one of the boys had yelled, 'I'm number 25 from Murray State,'" Jackson said. "My father had been so elated to tell us that a group of white boys wanted to be like me."

Campus life in general was changing in immeasurable ways. In the past, almost all of Murray State's students came from surrounding counties, but by 1963 the college had a Foreign Students Organization, headed by an Iraqi, to ease the transition of a growing number of students from all across the globe to life in Murray. Cultural life flourished, and one of the most cherished formal Murray State traditions, All Campus Sing, a spring group competition at Lovett Auditorium, took root in 1958. It has since grown to the point that its livestream now draws a global audience of Racer alumni along with heaving crowds of in-person spectators. ACS was joined in the mid-1960s by an informal (but equally endearing and enduring) tradition, that of happy Racer lovebirds adding mismatched footwear to the Shoe Tree on the campus quad to commemorate a wedding. Greek life flourished, creating early leadership opportunities for many of Murray State's most impressive late mid-century alumni. In sum, this was a period of great change and growth, wholly for the better, as Murray State matured into an institution more similar to the one we know today than the one it began as in 1923.

Up until the end of the war, aspiring local nurses acquired their craft under an ad hoc arrangement where they gained practical job skills through the Mason Memorial Hospital School of Nursing

Beanie-sporting Breds ponder a new name for a new decade.

while learning the fundamentals of physiology, chemistry, and nutrition in the classroom at Murray State. The closure of the hospital school in 1945 created an opportunity to formalize a new pre-nursing program on campus. Established in 1948, nursing has become one of Murray State's most popular majors.

Lynn Grove native and Murray State alumna Ruth E. Cole (1920–2014) became the college's first director of nursing education in January 1949. Captain Cole had served in the US Navy Nurse Corps during World War II and was recalled to active service when the Korean War broke out soon after she took up her position at Murray State. Under her guidance, the college's initial three-year diploma program evolved into a Bachelor of Science in nursing in 1964. The main auditorium in Mason Hall was named in Dr. Cole's honor.

Murray's William Mason Memorial Hospital was named for an early twentieth-century doctor whose wife and brother were also widely respected local physicians. Dr. Ora Kress Mason (1888–1970), wife to Will and sister-in-law to Rob, was most closely tied to Murray State, serving on the board of regents from 1928 to 1934. She was Murray's first female doctor, specializing in pediatrics and obstetrics, and was a beloved pillar of the community to hundreds of new parents. When the nursing program got a home of its own in the fall of 1967, Murray State honored her valued contributions to local medicine by naming it Mason Hall.

Murray State's business program grew considerably in the postwar years under Dr. Thomas Hogancamp (1922–93). Dr. Hogancamp joined the faculty in 1948 and became the chair of the Department of Commerce, forerunner to the Department of Business, in 1952. When a new business school was

One of the last classes of nurses to train at the Mason Memorial Hospital School, 1940.

Far left: Dr. Ruth E. Cole, director of nursing education.

Left: Dr. Ora K. Mason, physician, regent, and namesake of Mason Memorial Hospital/Mason Hall.

Dr. Thomas Hogancamp, first business dean.

Coach Harlan Hodges (1902–1994) led the men's basketball team into the Ohio Valley Conference era, winning its first regular season and tournament championships in 1951.

Engineer Johny B. Russell with a NASA lunar rover.

created in 1965 with separate departments for accounting and finance, business education and office administration, economics, management and general business, and marketing, Dr. Hogancamp served as its first dean. He oversaw the introduction of an MBA program in 1966, then became vice president for administrative affairs in 1968, and is the namesake of the General Services Building.

Alumnus Johny B. Russell (1924–2010) always had his eyes on the sky. This Hopkins County native joined the US Army Air Corps straight out of the Murray training school in 1942, then enrolled at Murray State College at the conclusion of his military service. He completed a B.S. in physics and mathematics, followed by a master's degree in 1950, taking a job after graduation at the Union Carbide Atomic Plant in Paducah, a state-of-the-art facility that enriched uranium fuel for military reactors and for use in nuclear weapons. Russell earned a reputation as one of the most talented and efficient engineers in the plant, opening up an exciting opportunity to do a different kind of cutting-edge work: aerospace.

The Boeing Company assigned Russell to the design and construction team building a lunar space rover, or "Moon Buggy," for NASA. These remarkable vehicles were lightweight at 460 pounds, battery-powered, and equipped for harsh terrain. They played an integral part in the Apollo 15, 16, and 17 missions from 1971 to 1972, and three of them remain on the surface of the moon. Later in the 1970s, Russell worked to develop the navigation system for the supersonic B-1 bomber, one of the most powerful aircraft in the US Air Force fleet during the Cold War. Murray State awarded Russell an honorary science doctorate in 2007 in recognition of his outstanding career in engineering. He donated his entire estate to fund scholarships and equipment for future generations of Murray State scientists.

Army ROTC cadets mustered in ranks.

Roughly a decade after hosting the war-era naval flight school, Murray State launched its US Army Reserve Officers' Training Corps (ROTC) program in 1952. For the next twenty years, its basic course was compulsory

| Game action at Racer Arena. |

for all male freshmen students, who underwent drilling in full uniform in a variety of open spaces across campus. Some cadets continued on to more specialized courses, and just over 1,000 ultimately graduated into careers in the army before the program closed in 1997. Murray State's ROTC was resurrected in 2004 and currently trains young recruits to serve as second lieutenants in the US Army, the Army Reserve, and the Army National Guard.

For over four decades, fans packed shoulder to shoulder in the longtime home of Murray State basketball, Racer Arena. This 5,500-seat facility opened just before Christmas in 1954 as the Fieldhouse and was known as one of the loudest and most intimidating places for opposing OVC teams to play. In 1998, the men's and women's basketball teams relocated to the new Regional Special Events Center (RSEC, now the CFSB Center), leaving the arena to the Racer women's volleyball team, which has continued to play there to the present day.

The Murray State athletics Racer nickname has its origins in practical, mid-century considerations. "Thoroughbred" chewed up a lot of letters in game reports in the sports section of local papers, so reporters started using T-breds, Breds, and Racers as shorthand. All three were used interchangeably through the 1950s, but college administrators liked Racers best and officially adopted it for every Murray State athletics team (except baseball) in 1961. Coach Johnny Reagan held out for tradition's sake, and he was such a legend here that athletics left baseball as the one holdout until 2014.

Alumnus Edward Craig Morris (1939–2006) was an archeologist who revolutionized our understanding of the Inca civilization, using excavation-based evidence that challenged the assumptions of his predecessors, who had mostly relied on written texts. Morris was born with a very serious heart condition, so his family encouraged him to focus his energies on reading and education, which suited him well. Morris graduated from the training school and then enrolled at Murray State, but his family later sold part of its 170-acre farm in east Calloway County to fund his transfer to Vanderbilt University, where he graduated magna cum laude in psychology and philosophy in 1961. Morris's fascination with the Inca began in the early 1960s while he was a graduate student at the University of Chicago. His extensive fieldwork revealed that the Inca empire was in fact a diverse collection of many high-altitude Andean ethnic groups, a find that cemented his reputation as one of the most respected scholars in his field. A brilliant but unassuming academic, Dr. Morris took several university teaching positions before joining the American Museum of Natural History in 1975, where he held a variety of roles from curator to vice president until his retirement in 2004.

John Mack Carter (1928–2014) was one of the most influential American magazine editors in the second half of the twentieth century, running the country's three most popular women's magazines, *McCall's* (1961–65), *Ladies' Home Journal* (1965–74), and *Good Housekeeping* (1975–94). Carter was a Murray native and cub reporter at the *Ledger and Times* who began his undergraduate studies at Murray State before transferring to the University of Missouri, where he completed a master's degree in journalism in 1949. Carter served two tours in the US Navy during the Korean War, then relocated to New York to launch his career as an editor.

Above, top: Dr. Craig Morris, renowned expert on Inca civilization.

Above, bottom: John Mack Carter, influential women's magazine editor.

Carter was convinced that American women's journals of the day often patronized their readers and badly needed a new tone, but he did not fully understand the challenges facing American women until over 100 feminists staged a high-profile eleven-hour sit-in—sometimes described as a hostage taking—at his *Ladies' Home Journal* office in March of 1970. Thereafter, Carter used his platform to advocate equal rights and draw attention to serious women's issues, including job discrimination and sexual harassment. Carter racked up a host of prestigious awards from journalism bodies and women's rights groups over his distinguished career. Murray State awarded him an honorary Doctor of Letters degree in 1971.

| Mary Ford Holland, grade school teacher and trailblazer. |

The Jim Crow system of racial segregation slowly began to crumble after World War II. Many Americans saw uncomfortable parallels with the policies of the defeated fascist powers, the spread of televised news made it more difficult for viewers to ignore stories about oppression, and it was harder for America to win Cold War allies abroad while its largest non-White minority was being persecuted at home. Dodgers legend Jackie Robinson integrated America's pastime in 1947, President Harry Truman desegregated the military in 1948 by executive order, and in 1954 the US Supreme Court made a monumental decision in the *Brown v. Board of Education* case that obliged schools, colleges, and universities across the country to desegregate. Before long, meaningful change came to communities big and small.

Trigg County native Mary Ford Holland (1907–99) integrated Murray State College in the summer of 1955 when she enrolled as a forty-eight-year-old nontraditional student. Ford already had a teaching certificate from West Kentucky Industrial School and over two decades of teaching experience in segregated one-room schools in Lyon County, but the *Brown* decision opened up new opportunities to upgrade her credentials. Holland had begun working toward a bachelor of science degree at the Kentucky State College for Negroes in Frankfort in 1941, but studying part-time at a considerable distance from campus slowed her progress. This prompted Holland to transfer to Murray State in 1955.

Dr. Woods and a handful of police officers personally escorted Holland to and from classes on her first day on the expectation that there would be resistance from her new White classmates, but the day passed without incident. This was a marked contrast to the pro-segregation protests and rioting that took place at other southern colleges in subsequent years. Holland later recalled one incident of racist abuse, but otherwise felt that she "wasn't too discriminated against." She continued teaching while she pursued her degree and ultimately graduated not long after the college's first Black alumna, Nancy Tyler Demartra, in 1961. Even though Holland integrated Murray State, she

returned to teaching in de facto segregated schools until the mid-1960s. In the final years before her retirement in 1972, she was a reading specialist at the integrated Lyon County Elementary School. In 1998, Holland was given the key to the city of Eddyville.

Despite the *Brown* decision, the OVC, Southeastern Conference, and American Athletic Conference were all still virtually Whites-only as late as the spring of 1960, but Murray State athletics was ready to make a long-overdue challenge to the status quo. The original plan was to begin by integrating the basketball team, but multisport talent and Murray native

| Dennis Jackson, Murray native and multisport star. |

Dennis Jackson transferred back home that same year from Alcorn A&M in Mississippi. Jackson became the first Black varsity athlete to compete for Murray State when he joined the track team for the 1960–1961 season, later running for one of the fastest college 4x100 meter relay teams in the southeast region. Jackson began as a walk-on his first year on the football team, but he earned a scholarship by his second for his stellar play as a receiver, tailback, and safety. He led the Racers in interceptions in 1962 (three), 1963 (five), and 1964 (four) and completed the 1964 season with an impressive nineteen catches for 349 yards and five touchdowns.

Jackson was a bona fide star who was readily accepted by his teammates, but he often encountered difficulty on the road as one of the first Black athletes in the OVC. Morehead had a Black player, Marshall Banks, on its 1959–1960 basketball team, but he was excluded from many away games and suffered the indignity of being left out of an official team photo. This was deeply hurtful, but his coach decided that it was easier than challenging racism directly. Jackson's experience at Murray State was very different. During a track meet at Middle Tennessee State College, a clerk at a segregated Murfreesboro hotel refused Jackson a bed for the night. He recalled, "We drove off and we had a meeting, and Coach [Bill] Furgerson said, 'We'll solve this.' We'll drive up, everybody will get out, and Jackson, you lay down in the back seat.' I laid down in the back seat till about twelve o'clock, when someone came and knocked on my window and snuck me in the hotel."

After completing undergraduate and master's degrees in education at Murray State, Jackson went on to teach physical education and health, in addition to coaching football, basketball, and track, in middle and high schools. He earned many honors for his sterling career as an educator and administrator, including Kentucky Colonel, Duke of Paducah, and Teacher of the Year at Paducah Middle School. He was inducted in the Murray State Athletics Hall of Fame in 2007, and the Dennis Jackson Racer Room at Stewart Stadium was dedicated in his honor in 2021.

Nancy Tyler Demartra was the first Black student to graduate from Murray State in May 1961, with a BA in elementary education, and was also the first to complete a master's degree two years later. She worked long hours around her classes at an off-campus job in Mayfield to pay for her education at Murray State, but she still found a way to play a defining role in the local civil rights movement.

In February 1960, Black college students in Greensboro, North Carolina, launched a wave of peaceful lunch counter sit-ins to protest segregated restaurant policies. They would typically order, be denied service, and were then often subjected to racist abuse by White patrons when they refused to leave. This tactic was incredibly effective in the age of television news because reporting on the sit-ins confronted Americans from coast to coast with the absurd reality that in many parts of the country a Black person could be arrested for simply attempting to order in a restaurant. Students across the country took inspiration from their Greensboro counterparts and embarrassed lunch counters across the Upper South into desegregating in rapid succession.

Nancy Tyler Demartra's senior yearbook photo, 1961.

The Hut, early 1960s.

The Hut was a cherished local hangout to most Racers, but it continued to deny service to Black patrons after Murray State desegregated in 1955. Demartra decided to take action in 1961, her senior year, leading a group that included five White allies who sat with her in the restaurant. When the cashier refused her money after a meal that her White friends had ordered, they all walked out together without paying. After three months of these protests, the Hut's management finally relented and agreed to serve Black patrons. After graduating, Demartra taught for three years in Paducah, then moved to teach in the Louisville and Jefferson County school districts. In 2010 she was inducted into the Kentucky Commission on Human Rights Hall of Fame for her lifetime of activism.

Second-year basketball coach Cal Luther (1927–2021) convinced Athletics Director Roy Stewart, President Ralph Woods, M. O. Wrather, and the college's board of regents in the spring of 1960 that the time had come for Murray State to actively recruit Black players. Luther's first was Tom Officer of Washington, Missouri, a gifted student and a talented player who put up 16.7 points per game for the college freshmen team over the 1961–1962 season. Officer was, unfortunately, subjected to merciless racist abuse on the court and ultimately withdrew from college after a fellow student hung him in effigy from a high-rise dorm window.

It was Stewart Johnson, a selfless, high-scoring forward from the Pittsburgh area who became the first Black varsity basketball player for Murray State when he suited up in 1963. The team had been in the midst of an uncharacteristically long run of relatively poor to middling seasons dating back to 1956–1957, but Johnson made an immediate positive impact and helped lead the Racers to their first NCAA tournament appearance in 1964. After his time at Murray State, he starred in the American Basketball Association for nine seasons, then finished his playing career in Europe. He was inducted into the Murray State Athletics Hall of Fame in 1979.

Basketball coach Cal Luther flanked by Hector Blondet (left) and Frank Streety (right).

Dr. Bob Burton, a 1962 alumnus and football standout, has had a long and distinguished career in the business and financial world. The All-OVC tackle was a 1962 draft pick by the San Francisco 49ers. After his playing days, Dr. Burton was the president, CEO, and chairman of several major public

Dr. Robert G. Burton Sr., captain of the 1962 football team.

A student gets some help from her dad moving into her dorm room before classes begin.

Lobby pay phones were rarely an ideal spot for private conversations, so residence dwellers cheered the introduction of dorm room telephones in 1963.

and private companies. He and his wife, Paula, funded the completion of the Burton Family Hall of Champions at the CFSB Center in 2015. Dr. Burton added, "without a Murray State football scholarship, I would not have been able to attend college. Murray State University was very good to me and gave me a platform to be successful in football and provided the discipline and necessary skills to be successful in business."

One of Murray State's most joy-filled traditions, All Campus Sing, began in 1958, on the quad-facing library steps. The music fraternity Sigma Alpha Iota launched this competition, which sees a variety of student organizations, including residence halls, fraternities, sororities, and independent clubs, perform choreographed musical numbers at a mass outdoor event every April. It is now held outside Lovett Auditorium. In-person All Campus Sing spectators have been joined in recent years by members of Racer Nation who watch by livestream from all over the world. The Murray State Alumni Association and the Office of Student Affairs have become cosponsors with Sigma Alpha Iota in recent years as the scale of the event grew larger. Many participants pay it forward by donating their surplus instruments to the music department's graduate program and to lower-income students who would like to pursue their musical interests.

In competition at All Campus Sing, 1960s.

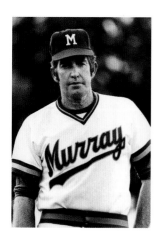

Legendary baseball coach Johnny Reagan, eleven-time OVC champion.

Murray State enjoyed its greatest baseball success under Missouri native Johnny Reagan (1926–2018), a legend who turned the Thoroughbreds into a regional powerhouse over his thirty-six-year run as coach. Reagan was a baseball and basketball star for Murray State in the mid-1940s who played briefly in the St. Louis Cardinals organization before turning to coaching full time. He took the helm at Murray State in 1958 and notched a superb career record of 776–508–11 (.599) by the time he retired in 1993.

Reagan won an OVC title in his first year as coach and never looked back. On his watch, the Breds had twenty-seven consecutive winning seasons and took eleven conference titles, climbing into the NCAA poll with top-thirty rankings on several occasions. This run of success earned him many accolades, including seven OVC Coach of the Year awards, as well as spots in the OVC, Murray State, American Baseball Coaches Association, Missouri Athletic, and Bismarck (Missouri) High School Halls of Fame. Two diamonds have been named in his honor, the field at Murray State and that of Bismarck High School, where he began his coaching career.

Raymond "Buddy" Hewitt (right), the longest tenured coach in Murray State history.

Raymond "Buddy" Hewitt (1929–2015) was a scrappy, undersized center for the great Breds football team that tied the Sul Ross Lobos in the 1949 Tangerine Bowl, but he's best known for a legendary forty-one-season run as the men's golf coach. "Big Bud" was a proud Racer alumnus who spent a half century at Murray State between his time as a student, instructor, and coach. Hewitt launched the Murray State men's golf team in 1961 and remained at its helm until 2001. He led his student athletes to a pair of OVC team championships, four OVC individual distinctions, and six All-America honors.

Nearly every first-time visitor to campus has questions when they first lay eyes on the dozens of mismatched pairs of shoes nailed to a tree on the campus quad. The Shoe Tree began in 1965 as a good luck ritual that stands as a testament to the hundreds of long, happy romantic matches that began on campus over the decades. When Racer couples marry, tradition obliges them to nail a pair of shoes to the tree, one from each partner. Many return later to add baby shoes as their families grow.

Winslow Cafeteria has fed hundreds of hungry undergrads every day during the academic year since it opened in 1964.

Eddyville native Bill Cunningham rose from the pre-law program at Murray State in 1966 all the way to a seat on the Kentucky Supreme Court forty years later. Justice Cunningham is known throughout western Kentucky as a passionate advocate for regional history and a prolific newspaper columnist and author, with six book credits to his name, including his well-received 1983 account *On Bended Knees: The True Story of the Night Rider Tobacco War in Kentucky and Tennessee*. Shortly after his graduation from Murray State, Cunningham served in the US Army for four years with the Judge Advocate General's Corps and was part of the team that negotiated with Hanoi and the Viet Cong over the terms of the peace settlement that ended the American phase of the Vietnam War. After returning home, he began a steady rise from Eddyville city attorney to circuit court judge and ultimately a Kentucky Supreme Court justice. Justice Cunningham's papers, including decades of correspondence with inmates he put away over the years, are found at Pogue Special Collections Library.

The Shoe Tree, a time-honored symbol of Racer love.

Few are remembered so fondly by so many as Alabama-born and Hopkinsville-raised Dr. Bob "Doc" McGaughey (1943–2019), a fixture in the journalism and mass communication department for almost fifty years. Doc graduated with honors in 1965, then did a stint in the army in Vietnam before coming back to Murray State to complete the first master's degree awarded by the journalism program. After completing his Ph.D. in mass communications at Ohio University, he returned to Murray State a second time to join the faculty. He served as department chair from 1974 to 1997, won a Max Carman Outstanding Teacher Award, and was an inductee into the Kentucky Journalism Hall of Fame, but he made his biggest impact as a warm, good-natured mentor to generations of his students.

Future Kentucky Supreme Court Justice Bill Cunningham, 1966.

Dr. Bob "Doc" McGaughey, stalwart of the journalism department.

| 4 |

The Boomers Come of Age

1966–1981

Introduction

A s Murray State approached the half-century mark, it was an institution that had undeniably come of age. This was partly the result of having reached the final stage in a rapid institutional progression from teachers' training school to college and ultimately to a university, but it also came from the addition of more sophisticated campus infrastructure. At a bureaucratic and organizational level, the creation of the Faculty Senate in 1974 gave a voice to instructors. Then the six schools were reconfigured into five colleges in 1975. These moves reflected the university's desire to strive for the best quality educational experience for both instructors and learners. At the same time, the great building boom of the late 1960s and early 1970s produced a new Fine Arts Building, home to a first-class art gallery, an intimate theatre for homegrown productions, and brand new campus radio and television studios. It also brought a landmark football stadium with seating for every student, faculty, and staff member, a fully equipped biology lab on Kentucky Lake, and, as a crowning achievement, the brand new Curris Center. By the early 1980s, Racer students had more and better options for both traditional and experiential learning, as well as great new outlets for culture and entertainment.

The university continued to make great progress during this period by offering new opportunities for women and Black students to fully participate in the campus experience via clubs and organizations, Greek life, and sports. The Women's Student Government Association was established during the 1966–1967 academic year to promote the interests of female students in a variety of ways, including a new freshman orientation program, but the most visible evidence of change came in the realm of athletics. In the 1960s, Murray State brought in a truly remarkable team of female physical education instructors who established a number of successful programs in rapid succession, often on a shoestring budget. It stands as a point of pride that the university rolled out a massive expansion of women's sport of its own volition well before the federal government mandated that colleges and universities across the nation offer equal opportunities in athletics in 1972.

Students Gene Murray and Linda Edwards celebrated the state legislature's decision to elevate Murray State to university status in 1966 with this improvised signage.

There were deeply significant advancements during this period for Black Racers as well, such as the first Black instructor, the hiring of the first full-time Black professor, and the first wave of dedicated campus and Greek organizations. This was the era of Jerry Sue Prichett and Walter Bumphus, two of our most distinguished alumni who both went on to long and successful careers as college administrators after graduation. There was also great symbolism to Prichett's 1968 election as Miss MSU in a campus-wide election by her peers. In the mid- to late 1950s, campus administrators had decided to actively pursue integration because it was the right thing to do. Within a decade, it was increasingly clear that the broader community of students, faculty, and staff had collectively decided to make Murray State a welcoming place for all comers.

This was also a great era of spirit and community. Greek organizations set up or expanded some of the longest running, and wackiest, campus activities to raise money for good causes. These included Sigma Chi's Derby Week, Alpha Gamma Rho's Paul Bunyan Day, and Lambda Chi Alpha's Watermelon Bust. Between Lovett Auditorium, Stewart Stadium, and Racer Arena, this was a high point for live entertainment, with campus performances from the likes of Kris Kristofferson, Waylon Jennings, Rush, Blue Oyster Cult, The Doobie Brothers, Jimmy Buffett, Molly Hatchet, and Brenda Lee. Two of our most cherished icons, mascot Dunker and an actual thoroughbred, Racer One, became staples of the fan experience at sporting events. The opening of the spacious new Curris Center in 1981 created a sprawling public venue for a mass celebration of the coming of the holiday season in a new fall tradition, the Hanging of the Green. These were admittedly trying times

Dr. Brinda Smith (back row, far right), physical education instructor and, later, trustee of the MSU Foundation, alongside a cast of pioneering coaches in women's athletics, late 1960s.

between an increasingly unpopular war in Vietnam, then a deep and long recession that challenged students and administrators to do more with less, but we came through it all together and became much stronger in the end.

Brinda Smith was a second-generation alumna who grew up on Murray State's campus, splitting much of her childhood between piles of books in the library and sprawling mud puddles on the east side of 15th Street. When an opportunity arose to teach at her alma mater, she joined the faculty in the fall of 1964 as a women's physical education instructor, a position she held until 1980. On her retirement, Dr. Smith launched a highly successful second career as an accredited financial advisor and gave sage guidance to the MSU Foundation Board of Trustees for many years. Her generous gift funded the 2019 renovation of the Smith-Johnson Genealogy and History Room in her old haunt, Pogue Library, a tribute to her mother, Mary Johnson Smith, a longtime Calloway teacher, and her aunt, Lieutenant Commander Anna Mayrell Johnson, a political science professor and dean of women who served as a navy pilot in World War II.

The landmark event in the history of women's college athletics was Title IX of the Education Amendments Act of 1972, which mandated that institutions receiving federal funds must provide equal opportunities for women in sports. Murray State had in fact already begun offering new outlets for female student athletes, thanks to the efforts of a dynamic generation of women coaches. Murray State made tennis its first new addition in 1967 under Nita Head, Margaret Simmons established track and field in 1968 and then cross-country three years later, women's basketball was resurrected in 1971 with Depression-era star Dew Drop Rowlett in charge, and then volleyball was added the following year. A second wave of new women's sports came a generation later, including golf in 1994, soccer in 2000, and softball in 2008.

Beaming on the shoulders of her teammates is Carla Coffey, a track and basketball star from 1967 to 1971 who became

Volleyball was one of several women's sports added in the late 1960s and early 1970s.

the first woman inducted in the Racer Athletics Hall of Fame in 1981. Her right hand is on the shoulder of fellow Hall of Famer Margaret Simmons, a six-time OVC Coach of the Year and two-time Kentucky Women's Athletic Conference Coach of the Year who had a wildly successful run from 1967 to 1991.

Philanthropy is a major part of Greek life, and a new slate of fun activities for serious causes took root in the 1960s and 1970s as fraternities and sororities grew

Carla Coffey (top center) and Coach Margaret Simmons (bottom center).

along with the university. The Sigma Chi fraternity established its Epsilon Tau chapter at Murray State in April 1959 and soon after launched Derby Week as an annual fundraiser for the Wallace Village in Colorado, a rehabilitation school for children suffering brain injuries, and, later, the local Champs Program. A typical Derby Week began with cash collecting, then progressed into inter-Greek competitions, including a scavenger hunt and the Derby Chase, which challenged sorority members to nick derby hats from Sigma Chi brothers. The week concluded, of course, with a series of themed parties.

Alpha Gamma Rho set up its Alpha Omega chapter on campus in 1968 and followed with Paul Bunyan Day, named for the lumberjack giant of North American folklore, to raise money for the Cystic Fibrosis Foundation. This was a mud-spattered, full country competition that included a greased pig chase, tug o' war, caber tossing, log sawing, and nail hammering, just as one would expect from an agriculture fraternity.

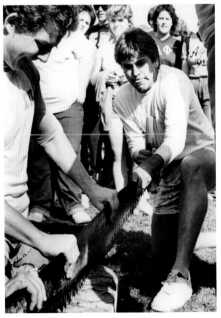

Sigma Chi's Derby Week, 1970s

Alpha Gamma Rho's Paul Bunyan Day, 1970s.

| President Harry Sparks (center). |

Dr. Harry Sparks (1907–96) followed a career path similar to Murray State's great early and mid-twentieth-century leaders, beginning modestly as a schoolroom instructor, accumulating degrees, moving into the roles of principal and district supervisor, then capping a long and distinguished career by serving as a university president. This Rockcastle County native rose to the rank of lieutenant commander in the US Navy during World War II, training allied Soviet and Chinese troops how to spot enemy warplanes, then he joined the education faculty at Murray State in 1948 after having completed his doctorate at UK. He became department head in 1952, then president of the Kentucky Education Association in 1960, and state superintendent of public instruction in 1963, earning a Kentucky-wide reputation as a tireless supporter of teachers and schools along the way.

| Jerry Sue Pritchett, Miss MSU, 1968. |

Dr. Sparks, an energetic, good-humored, and experienced administrator, was the regents' unanimous choice to follow Dr. Woods as Murray State's fifth president. His tenure, 1968 to 1973, came at a time of tremendous campus unrest across the nation as Baby Boomer students grew impatient over the ongoing war in Vietnam coupled with slow progress on a variety of pressing issues, including civil and women's rights. Relatively benign sit-in student occupations were extremely common on campuses across the country during this period, but violence sometimes erupted at protests and lives were lost, most tragically at Kent State University in Ohio and Jackson State College in Mississippi. One of Dr. Sparks's most important accomplishments as president was keeping the peace in troubled times, made possible in large part due to his patient willingness to listen to his students' concerns and to channel their youthful energy toward debate and peaceful demonstration rather than destructive forms of confrontation.

Hopkins County native Jerry Sue Thornton (née Pritchett) was a first-generation college student who became the first Black graduate student to teach at Murray State in 1969 while she was working on her M.A. in communications. She was widely popular with her classmates, winning the campus-wide election for the Miss MSU crown in 1969. After completing her Ph.D. at the University of Texas at Austin, Dr. Thornton taught, served as a dean, then rose to the rank of president at two different community colleges over the course of an outstanding career in academia.

Murray State students and faculty had been putting together radio broadcasts as early as 1948, but the Federal Communications Commission's 1969 decision to grant a permit for WKMS to operate at 91.3 on the FM dial opened up the possibility of something both more permanent and professional. The fledgling station launched its first official broadcast from its cramped two-room home in Wilson Hall on May 11, 1970, but Dr. Ray Mofield (1921–95) raised enough funds over its first year on the air to build modern, fully equipped studios on the top floor of the new Price Doyle Fine Arts Building. For over fifty years, Murray State's National Public Radio affiliate has been one of our most trusted sources for news, information on local events, and great music.

WKMS's first broadcast with President Sparks and Dr. Mofield.

Ernest T. Brooks (1942–2012) was a veteran of the civil rights movement in his hometown, Jackson, Tennessee, where he was a two-term president of the Jackson-Madison County NAACP. His outspoken role in the fight against Jim Crow as a student activist at Lane College closed teaching opportunities to him after graduation, so he taught in Missouri before pursuing a doctorate in counselor education at The Ohio State University. After completing his degree, Dr. Brooks joined the guidance and counseling department in 1970 as Murray State's first full-time Black professor. As an undergraduate at Lane he was a member of the Omega Psi Phi Fraternity, and he later chartered its Alpha Beta chapter at Murray State in 1971.

Dr. Ernest T. Brooks, Murray State's first Black professor.

By the 1970s, a pair of groups took root to give a campus voice to Black students and to assist incoming Racers. The first was the Black Student Union in the 1970–1971 academic year, followed by the Black Advisory Council in 1973. The BAC ran a full slate of social events, including fall term orientation, a Homecoming Pageant, and Black History Month programming every February.

Black Advisory Council members, 1973–1974.

Dr. Walter Bumphus (right), first director of minority affairs.

Dr. Walter Bumphus came to Murray State as an undergraduate in 1966 from Caldwell County High, earning a bachelor's degree in speech communication and then a master's degree in guidance and counseling before leaving in 1971 to pursue a Ph.D. in higher education administration at the University of Texas at Austin. Along with his former classmate Dr. Jerry Sue Thornton, he became an accomplished community college administrator. A champion of access, affordability, and diversity, he became president and CEO of the American Association of Community Colleges in 2010. Both of his alma maters awarded him distinguished graduate status, and he served on Murray State's board of regents from 2016 to 2018.

Racer Band, a mainstay since the founding era.

Murray State has offered high-quality music instruction all the way back to its first day of classes in 1923, adding a band class the following year once Geneve Wells, an accomplished pianist and Rainey T. Wells's daughter, joined the faculty. It appears that Murray State fielded its first band in 1926, adding its signature blue and gold uniforms the following year. Within a decade it had grown to eighty players and had ventured into swing dance and a marching band, befitting tastes of the era. In the intervening decades, the Racer Band has become such a campus fixture that it has become nearly as much of a draw at football and basketball games as the actual sporting event itself.

Murray State's deep theatre roots go all the way back to the Sock and Buskin Club in the founding era. In more recent decades, hundreds of talented student actors have honed their craft on the stage of the Robert Johnson Theatre in the Price

Student production at the Robert Johnson Theatre.

| Art auction at the Clara Eagle Art Gallery, 1970s. |

Doyle Fine Arts Building. The theatre opened in 1971, giving student actors the first dedicated campus space of their own. Named for the university's long-serving theatre chair, it has 344 seats, full dressing rooms and laundry facilities, as well as a workshop for set designers. The theatre department typically runs a half dozen productions every year.

Nestled into 4,000 square feet on the sixth and seventh floors of the Price Doyle Fine Arts Building is the Clara Eagle Art Gallery, one of the finest gems on campus. The gallery is named for Clara M. Eagle, who taught art at Murray State from 1946 until the early 1970s and was a longtime department chair. The gallery hosts roughly a half dozen exhibits every year featuring the best work from Murray State students and rotating loans from other talented artists from all over the country. One of the highlights of the spring calendar is the annual Murray State Art Auction, which gives the community an opportunity to support our students.

With an eye to serving the nation as it had during World War II, Murray State added its military science program as Cold War tensions deepened in the late 1940s. The ROTC came soon after, while the Korean War was raging on the other side of the Pacific. President Woods, himself an army veteran of World War I, had committed Murray State to two years of mandatory ROTC training for male students in 1952, but the program had become

| Colonel Eff Birdsong, professor of military science. |

Murray State alumnus, Joe Staton.

May 1968 cover art for *The Fuze* by Joe Staton.

a lightning rod for dissent by the time Colonel Eff Weeks Birdsong Jr. (1922–2004) joined the military science faculty at the height of the Vietnam War in 1967. To defuse these tensions, the board of regents first rolled the ROTC requirement back to one year in 1969, then made the program entirely voluntary in 1971. Colonel Birdsong, a Texan and highly decorated combat veteran of World War II and the Korean War, threw his support behind the move toward an all-volunteer approach to the campus ROTC.

The counterculture of the 1960s most definitely found its way to campus, as evidenced by a number of underground newspapers that circulated in competition to the university-sanctioned *Murray State News*. Mastheads changed and publication schedules were erratic, but these papers provided an outlet to antiwar activists and a broader coalition of fellow travelers who wanted to vent their concerns about diverse issues all the way down to the local level. Seen here is page 1 from the May 1968 issue of *The Fuze* featuring artwork from North Carolina native Joe Staton. After he graduated from Murray State in 1970, he began his career as a cartoonist in 1971 at Charlton Comics, then worked for both Marvel and DC Comics over the course of the decade. Longtime fans of *Justice Society of America, Green Lantern, Dick Tracy, Scooby-Doo, Richie Rich,* and *Casper the Friendly Ghost* are all familiar with his art. His work was recognized with an Inkpot Award at Comic-Con in 1983, and more recently he and writer Mike Curtis won the Best Syndicated Strip Harvey Award three times for their efforts on *Dick Tracy*.

The Student Government Association's response to the highly polarized climate of the Nixon era was to plan Murray State's most ambitious lecture series ever. Insight '71 was supposed to draw a range of high-profile speakers from the political left and right, representing views from academia, media, the law, and civic activism.

Far left: Students anticipate the Insight '71 lecture series.

Left: William Kunstler speaking on WGBH's *The Advocates* television show, April 20, 1972. Photo courtesy of UMass Amherst Special Collections and University Archives.

The SGA and the board of regents clashed, however, over the inclusion of the controversial lawyer William Kunstler, who was fresh off a trial victory in his defense of the Chicago Seven on charges of conspiracy to start a riot at the Democratic National Convention in 1968. To Kunstler's supporters, his inclusion cut to the heart of freedom of speech, but his detractors saw the proposed event as a prelude to rioting in their peaceful college town.

Off campus, public opinion was firmly opposed to Kunstler's upcoming visit, leading the board of regents to revoke his speaking contract on February 2. Many students saw this as a heavy-handed form of censorship and protested for weeks until Mayor Holmes Ellis and Judge Robert O. Miller worked up a clever plan where Kunstler could come to Murray in March without the formal blessing of the university. Three of the Insight '71 invitees chose not to participate in the series, but Kunstler did ultimately come to Murray, speaking before an off-campus crowd on the courthouse lawn rather than a much larger one in Lovett Auditorium. This compromise left no one fully satisfied, but it did succeed in lowering the political temperature.

Conducting research at Hancock Biological Station.

The establishment of Hancock Biological Station on Kentucky Lake in 1972 gave Murray State science students the opportunity to conduct comprehensive field-based research and learning on aquatic and terrestrial habitats from a fully equipped laboratory just sixteen miles east of the main campus. The station was named for longtime biology chair Dr. Hunter Hancock (1910–2003).

Lambda Chi Alpha came to campus with its Lambda Eta chapter in 1968, adding the annual fall Watermelon Bust to the Greek social calendar in 1973. As per tradition, the festivities kicked off with the ceremonial dropping of a watermelon from the roof of Elizabeth Hall. Over the course of the day, the Bust pitted teams from sororities along with those drawn from dormitory residents against each other in a watermelon relay and a seed-spitting competition, among other activities.

Lambda Chi Alpha's Watermelon Bust.

Robert Danielson, a co-owner of The Big Apple in Puryear, Tennessee, a popular spot for "Going South."

While most of the nation discarded Prohibition with gusto in 1933, the city of Murray held on to this unpopular social experiment until the year 2000, and then only slightly let up by granting restaurants the right to sell individual drinks. There was one solution for legions of nonteetotalers during the intervening years, however: "going south." The road to Paris just across the state line in Tennessee was lined with character establishments that served the needs of thirsty Racers, including 641 Club, The Big Apple, and Katmandu. The Big Apple Cafe decided to go north from Puryear in 2001, making life much easier on its loyal Calloway customers by opening a new location in Murray on Arcadia Circle. Wet forces finally prevailed in a 2012 referendum that put Murray's alcohol laws more in line with the rest of the country.

Following Dr. Sparks's retirement in 1973, the board of regents put Murray State in the hands of a dynamic new president, Constantine "Deno" Curris, who began his work here at the tender age of thirty-two. Curris was a wunderkind Lexington native whose academic career had been advancing at warp speed. A graduate of UK and the University of Illinois, he joined Midway College at age twenty-four as vice president and dean of faculty while he was working toward his Ed.D. in higher education at UK. Dr. Curris was the director of academic programs for the West Virginia Board of Education by 1968, the following year he became dean of student personnel programs at Marshall

President Constantine Curris and daughter Elena.

University, and then in 1971 he became vice president and dean of the faculty at the West Virginia Institute of Technology. He was somehow both highly experienced and the youngest university president in Kentucky when Murray State hired him in September 1973.

Murray State had already staked its claim as a successful regional university with a number of signature programs, so Dr. Curris set his priorities to boosting overall quality as a means of attracting and retaining capable faculty and high-achieving students. He was also determined to fine-tune programs to better meet the public's needs. There were many successes along the way, perhaps most notably the construction of a brand new university center that bears his name, along with unforeseen challenges. The stagnant economy of the post–Vietnam War and 1973 oil shock era, coupled with the demographics of a shrinking student pool as the tail end of the massive Baby Boom generation came of age, brought the era of generous state support for public education to an end by the

Roy Stewart Stadium has been the home of Racer football since 1973. The Racers' terrific 9–2–1 season in 1979 was highlighted by a 24–7 homecoming victory over the rival EKU Colonels.

The game was broadcast live on ABC-TV.

early 1980s. Cooperation between President Curris and some members of the board of regents broke down in 1981 under the stresses brought on by the need to impose painful budget cuts, resulting in his departure.

After ten years at Murray State, Dr. Curris went on to serve as president of the University of Northern Iowa and Clemson University, then spent nearly a decade as president of the American Association of State Colleges and Universities before retiring in 2008. The following year he came back to Murray State to serve as chair of the board of regents, helping steer the university through a new presidential search. In the later years of his presidency at Murray State, Dr. Curris was frequently seen riding bikes on campus with his daughter, Elena Diane Curris (1977–2015), who went on to become a successful university administrator in her own right at California State University, Long Beach.

Right, top: MSU-TV Channel 11 launched in the 1974–1975 academic year, giving students experience as on-air reporters, camera operators, audio mixers, and lighting technicians.

Right, bottom: Judge David Buckingham swearing in as the second Racer to sit on the Kentucky Supreme Court, 2019. Photo courtesy of the *Murray Ledger and Times.*

Bob Valentine, actor, instructor, and stand-up comic.

Longtime St. Louis Cardinals coach Mark Riggins delivers batting practice. Photo courtesy of the St. Louis Cardinals.

A Breds baseball game, 1970s.

Doc McGaughey was one half of "the Bobs," and the other was his longtime friend, colleague, and fellow bon vivant Bob Valentine. The New York-born Valentine joined the journalism and mass communications faculty in 1974, but over the following decades he applied his varied interests to teach a range of courses, from advertising to theatre, earning multiple wins as best faculty member in student polls along with a more formal nod as Max Carman Outstanding Teacher in 2016. Beyond the classroom, he is known as an accomplished regional theatre player and stand-up comedian.

Southpaw Mark Riggins out of Loogootee, Indiana, was one of the most talented pitchers on some of the all-time greatest Breds baseball teams in the late 1970s. He played five seasons of professional baseball in the St. Louis Cardinals organization, then embarked on a thirty-year coaching career that took him to the highest levels of the game. Riggins became the Cardinals pitching coach in 1995, later serving in the same role for the Chicago Cubs in 2011 and the Cincinnati Reds in 2016. These assignments were interspersed with stints as a minor league pitching coordinator in all three organizations. Riggins retired after the 2018 season so he could return to Murray year-round and spend more time with his wife, Tammie, who was a valued member of the MSU Foundation team for almost twenty years. The foundation honored her dedicated service by establishing the Tammie Riggins Memorial Scholarship in 2020 to help high-performing Murray High students.

Coach Johnny Reagan twice took his Breds to the NCAA Division I baseball championship, which then pitted the top thirty-four college teams against each other. His 1975 team had a 40–9 regular season record and the 1979 squad finished 27–10–2. The 1979 Breds made the deepest push in the NCAA championship in Murray State history, beating Tulane and New Orleans in the first

Beloved campus mascot Dunker has been entertaining fans since 1976.

Violet Cactus, the original Racer One, takes a touchdown lap.

two rounds of the South Regional before falling to powerhouse Mississippi State.

Fully befitting Kentucky's long and proud equine traditions, Racer One and an accompanying jockey have taken a celebration lap on the Marshall Gage Track after every home touchdown scored at Stewart Stadium since 1976. Violet Cactus became the first Racer One after she was donated to the university's equine program following an injury that prematurely ended her racing career. She was laid to rest in 1984 near the north end zone, the starting position for all of her many victory laps over the years. This unique tradition has evolved, and Racer One duties now rotate periodically to a new horse and student jockey pair.

Calf roping at the Cherry Expo Center.

Murray State added the West Kentucky Livestock and Exposition Center (later renamed the William "Bill" Cherry Agricultural Exposition Center) next to the University Farm complex in 1976, creating a perfect space for regional livestock shows, Future Farmers of America (FFA) Day, and tractor pulls, among other events. The Cherry Expo Center is also home to the university's accomplished rodeo team, which began competing there immediately after it opened.

Alpha Tau Omega's Zeta Lambda chapter, established in 1959, proved that there were still plenty of good ideas left for uniquely bizarre Greek events

Alpha Tau Omega's Frog Hop.

Murray State University
Dedication Ceremonies for the Harry Lee Waterfield Library
September 2, 1978, 2:00 p.m. (C.D.T.)

when it came up with the Frog Hop in 1978. ATO gave each competing sorority team a frog, and it was each team's responsibility to train its loaner amphibian for race day. The event was capped, naturally, by a group meal of fried frog legs washed down with "swamp water."

Even with the addition of the Lowry Library Annex building next door in the mid-1960s, the original library on 15th Street had become too cramped to accommodate the needs of a rapidly growing student body. This prompted university libraries to take over the Waterfield Student Union Building, which became Waterfield Library in the fall of 1978. The namesake to both iterations is Calloway native Harry Lee Waterfield (1911–88), an alumnus, newspaper publisher, former regent, state legislator, Kentucky speaker of the House, two-time lieutenant governor of Kentucky, and insurance executive.

Alumni who attended during the later 1960s and 1970s can attest that one of the major consequences of rapid growth was overcrowding in the Student Union Building. In January 1981, Murray State solved that problem when it opened the doors to the 135,000-square-foot, four-story Curris Center. In its early years, this new campus hub was home to a range of popular amenities, including spacious meeting rooms, a ballroom, a bowling alley, a pool hall, a movie theater, an arcade, several new dining options, a dramatically expanded university store, and a more intimate venue for small concerts and stand up comedy at the Stable Doors.

Former Kentucky Lieutenant Governor Harry Lee Waterfield.

Curris Center, the new campus hub.

The annual Hanging of the Green is an English-style holiday tradition that originated in the late 1970s in the Ordway Hall dormitory. It moved to the Curris Center in 1981, adding a thirty-foot cedar tree from the Tennessee Valley Authority.

| 5 |

Innovation and Modernization

1981–1997

Introduction

T HE LAST TWO DECADES OF THE TWENTIETH CENTURY brought Americans two painful recessions, the rapid spread of personal computing, and the dawn of the Internet age—disruptions that changed nearly every facet of our daily lives and inevitably spilled over onto campus. Generally, the pace quickened, competition heated up, and self-reliance became more important than ever. In the end, considerable positive change came from the university's creative efforts to provide new opportunities for students on campus and beyond, to use its resources to plant deeper roots through western Kentucky, and, finally, to reimagine the entire residential experience in a life-changing way for its undergraduates.

Evolution and growth were evident all around us during this period, perhaps most symbolically in the office of the president, where Dr. Kala Stroup took over in 1983 as the first woman to lead any university in Kentucky. Dr. Stroup was an inspiration to women, living proof that they could break the glass ceiling in pursuit of career opportunities that were effectively closed during their parents' generation.

On a functional day-to-day level, new technology was everywhere. Computer labs popped up across campus, but student appreciation for the PCs of the 1980s was never greater than on registration day. Registration was once a grueling summer ordeal where thousands of sweat-soaked students snaked through hours-long lines at Racer Arena before they could sit down face to face with an advisor who would place them in classes using handmade ledgers. The introduction of PCs sped the process dramatically, paving the way for today's pain-free and near-instantaneous online registration. During the 1990s, Murray State also staked its claim on the World Wide Web with its first site, www.mursuky.edu, a mashup of Murray State University and Kentucky.

In terms of physical growth, Murray State added considerable and varied infrastructure stretching all the way from the Mississippi River to the city of Hopkinsville. The state transferred the Breathitt Veterinary Center in Hopkinsville to university control in 1982, providing a massive boost to the pre-veterinary science program in the form of sprawling, state-of-the-art laboratories for research and instruction. The following year Western Baptist Hospital in Paducah turned over the richest cultural site in the Purchase Area, the 700-year-old former Mississippian community at Wickliffe Mounds, to the university so its archeology team could manage preservation efforts and modernize dig procedures. That fall, area golfers cheered the opening of Miller Memorial Golf Course, launched as a first-class university-operated facility just outside of the city thanks to the great generosity of the Miller family. In 1991, the newly opened Collins Industry and Technology Center provided ample space to expand engineering technology, the increasingly popular occupational health and safety program, and other offerings.

In entertainment and sports, many of our students made their first mark on campus during this period before moving on to professional careers that brought them national acclaim. Murray State's theatre department has cultivated so many talented players over the years, none greater than the legendary W. Earl Brown, an actor whose career highlight list is too long to mention here. In athletics, Pat Spurgin was the first Racer to bring home an Olympic medal, winning the gold in women's rifle at the Summer Games in Los Angeles in 1984. At the end of the decade, Popeye Jones dominated the OVC and brought hardwood glory to the Racers, then went on to play more NBA games than any of our former players. Around the same time over on the diamond, Kirk Rueter unlocked his prodigious talents under Coach Reagan, proving himself as the greatest Murray State baseball player ever after pitching through thirteen productive major league seasons.

The Racer community reliably held fast in good times and bad. The opening of Tent City in 1989 as a pre-homecoming football game tailgate party marked a brand new tradition, one that allowed Racers past and present to connect with each other and the university. When one of us was down, we picked each other up, as evidenced by the response to the news that undergraduate Stacy Sommer had been diagnosed with a form of leukemia that left her with the slimmest hope of survival. Campus groups and Greek organizations rallied fundraising efforts to help cover part of her medical expenses, and her plight motivated hundreds of Racers to donate blood in search of a marrow match on campus. Sommer miraculously survived the ordeal, married, had a daughter, and helped manage a family business back home in Rockford, Illinois. In 2011, Tri Sigma invited her back to campus for an alumni gathering that included the initiation ceremony she had missed out on in 1988.

President Kala Stroup, daughter Megan, husband Joe, and son Chandler.

A university is many things to many people. It is a home base for faculty members to conduct research and hone the craft of teaching as well as a source of jobs for hundreds of dedicated staff members who do less visible but equally important work maintaining operations in a variety of crucial ways. But first and foremost, it is a place for students to learn, to grow, and to prepare themselves to lead rich, independent lives. For those who work with them, the greatest source of satisfaction comes when students unlock their potential and find their passion. To that end, Murray State took a pair of major initiatives in the 1990s.

The world had been coming to Murray State in significant numbers since the 1960s, and by the 1990s it became time to formalize and expand programs that would take a growing number of Racers out into the world. Belizeans had been coming to Murray State since 1992, and the education department began a highly popular teaching exchange program in Belize in 2007. This helped cultivate a very special relationship with an English-speaking Caribbean country and opened the perspective of education majors beyond our borders. Similarly, but for a broader audience, Murray State partnered with Universität Regensburg in eastern Bavaria to create its flagship study abroad program out of a centrally located base that continues to allow intrepid Racers broad opportunities to explore continental Europe.

Back at home, the biggest and most dramatic change was the introduction of the residential college system in 1997, an initiative brought in by the president, Dr. Kern Alexander. This move was inspired by the most venerable English institutions, Oxford and Cambridge, which have for centuries grouped their students into residential colleges that form their own unique traditions and create extracurricular opportunities to engage with faculty members, to compete in sports, and to generally deepen small community bonds through a variety of engaging activities. This popular innovation directed incoming Racers, residence dwellers and commuters, into one of eight colleges: Clark, Elizabeth, Hart, Hester, Regents, Richmond, Springer-Franklin, and White. At the time, few would have predicted the sometimes isolating consequences of the growth of Internet culture or the divisions created by an increasingly fragmented and politically siloed media landscape, but the residential college system was a ready-built antidote that brought new Racers together in a special way.

Another dynamic young administrator, Dr. Kala Stroup, took the reins at Murray State in 1983 and led the university through to the end of the decade. Dr. Stroup was a Jayhawk through and through, completing a B.A. in speech and drama, an M.S. in educational psychology, and a Ph.D. in speech communication all at the University of Kansas before embarking on an eighteen-year career as a

Alpha Gamma Deltas rocking through the night in Curris Center chairs to raise money for juvenile diabetes, 1986.

professor, advisor, and dean of women at her alma mater prior to her arrival in Murray. Dr. Stroup's appointment at Murray State made her the first female college or university president anywhere in Kentucky, a huge milestone for women educators across the state.

Stroup's primary goal as president was to continue Dr. Curris's efforts to promote academic quality, but she also outlined a number of new priorities, such as putting more emphasis on the adult learner, collaborating with other universities, and developing a strategic plan. Her tenure was highlighted by construction of the Collins Industry and Technology Center and approval for the introduction of Murray State classes at Paducah Community College. She was succeeded by Dr. Ron Kurth, a retired rear admiral, Sovietologist, and former defense attache in Cold War Moscow.

Alpha Gamma Delta's popular Rock-A-Thon originated in the early 1980s as part of the sorority's efforts to raise money for juvenile diabetes. The most popular components of the event were a lip-synch battle and a raucous Family Feud-style competition pitting rival fraternities against each other. The "rock" in the event title refers to a twenty-four-hour rocking chair session for chapter members in the Curris Center to raise awareness for a good cause. In recent years, Alpha Gamma Delta has turned proceeds over to hunger-based charities such as Meals on Wheels and Feeding America.

Concentrating on a putt at Miller Memorial Golf Course.

L. D. Miller (1913–92) was a farm boy from just outside Coldwater who graduated from Murray State in 1937, made his mark in business, then gave back to his beloved alma mater in a truly innovative way during his later years. His wife, Frances, was an avid golfer, and he wanted to create a fitting tribute to her memory after she passed in 1976, so three years later he donated his family farm to the MSU Foundation on the stipulation that it be developed into an eighteen-hole course named for his late wife within a decade. The par-71 course, just six miles east of the main campus, opened well ahead of schedule and to great critical acclaim, winning recognition from the American Society of Golf Course Architects as one of the best-designed in the country. The first group of golfers hit the tees on Memorial Day weekend in 1983, and thousands have enjoyed playing the course every year since. The Murray State golf team has perhaps been the greatest beneficiary, practicing at a first-class home course with a wide variety of challenging holes for almost forty years. In 2016, the Miller family followed up with another major gift of over $1 million to sustain maintenance costs and upgrades at the course.

In 1977, Murray State acquired one of its signature regional facilities, the Breathitt Veterinary Center in Hopkinsville, to bolster its animal science program. UK originally opened the Animal Diagnostic Laboratory in Hopkinsville in 1967, then passed it to the Kentucky Department of Agriculture. Governor Julian Carroll in turn transferred it to Murray State to maximize its potential. Work began soon thereafter on a new building that was dedicated as the Edward T. Breathitt Veterinary Center in late November 1982. The new center featured modern facilities, including a surgery room, airtight testing labs, and a variety of research amenities, including classrooms for hands-on instruction. The center's primary mandate was to help Kentucky farmers solve mystery animal ailments, and in so doing to boost the state's multi-billion-dollar agricultural sector.

In 2017, Murray State opened a new, upgraded 77,000-square-foot Breathitt Veterinary Center that is accredited by the American Association of Veterinary Laboratory Diagnosticians. It has

Alpha Sigma Alpha's Beta Nu chapter has run Teeter for Tots to benefit a variety of children's charities over the years.

Murray State archeology team, Wickliffe Mounds.

the only Biosafety Level III suite in the state. The center, now part of the Hutson School of Agriculture, provides rapid, high-accuracy animal disease testing for the livestock, poultry, and equine industries in Kentucky as well as neighboring Missouri, Tennessee, Illinois, and Indiana. The USDA National Animal Health Laboratory Network designated it as one of just twenty-three Level 1 laboratories in the country in early 2021.

Roughly 700 to 900 years ago, Mississippian mound builders farmed and traded out of a burgeoning community on a bluff overlooking the Mississippi River just thirty miles west of Paducah. We now know it as Wickliffe Mounds. For reasons that remain unknown, the village was abandoned in the late fourteenth century, long before contact with Euro-American explorers and settlers. Americans did not get their first hint of the site's rich history until state surveyors mapped the era in the late 1880s. Paducah lumber baron Colonel W. Fain King purchased the surrounding land and began digging for relics in the 1930s for a tourist attraction he named the "Ancient Buried City," but his ambitions ultimately outstripped his resources. He donated the site to Western Baptist Hospital in 1946, which in 1983 handed it over to Murray State so preservation efforts and archeological surveys could be conducted in a more professional manner. In recognition of the site's great significance to the indigenous peoples of the Americas, Murray State ultimately transferred the Wickliffe

Mounds Historic Site to the Kentucky Department of Parks in 2004. Visitors today can learn about Mississippian peoples by viewing an excavated ceremonial mound and touring a popular museum with interpretive exhibits built around artifacts discovered on the site.

Pi Kappa Alpha's Epsilon Lambda chapter was the first national social fraternity installed on campus in 1958. Mr. MSU Alan Zacharias leads the Pikes at 1983's All Campus Sing.

Freakers Ball, the 1980s–1990s-era
Halloween party at the Curris Center.

W. Earl Brown was a farm-raised, first-generation college student who arrived at Murray State with a love of movies and big dreams of Hollywood. He discovered his talent for acting on the stage of the Robert Johnson Theatre, starring first in the 1983 production of *That Championship Season,* and he never looked back. After graduation, he headed north to Chicago to complete an MFA at the DePaul University Theatre School, honing his craft on the stage alongside Gillian Anderson and John C. Reilly. He was discovered by director Wes Craven following a move to Los Angeles in 1993, and the "Master of Horror" cast him in a string of his box office hits, including 1996's *Scream.* Brown's long list of credits is tied together by one theme: highly memorable turns in some of the best film and television productions of recent decades. Most fans would argue that his most iconic role was that of the menacing enforcer Dan Dority on HBO's much beloved western *Deadwood* from 2004 to 2006 and again for a follow-up film in 2019.

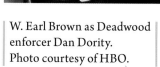

W. Earl Brown as Deadwood
enforcer Dan Dority.
Photo courtesy of HBO.

Nikki Millan, Alpha Phi Alpha's
Miss Black and Gold, 1989.

Alpha Phi Alpha established Zeta Omicron, the first chapter of a historically Black fraternity at Murray State, in 1969. Alpha Phi Alpha draws crowds in the hundreds for its annual Miss Black and Gold pageant, which was added to the Greek social calendar in the mid-1980s. The crown came with a scholarship and the opportunity to advance to regional and national competitions.

Murray State turned to one of its own alumni, Walter Bumphus, to serve as its first director of minority affairs in 1972, a time when few other post-secondary institutions offered the position. The university followed this move by creating the Minority Student Affairs Office in 1984 to increase Black enrollment and retention. In its early years, the office focused on pairing incoming freshmen and transfers with mentors who could help them smoothly transition into campus life. MSA's efforts were not simply one way; it devoted considerable energy to educate the majority student population on the culture and experiences of the growing body of Black students, primarily through Black History Month programming and a variety of community projects. Over the years, the center has evolved into African American Student Service and Ethnic Programs, then the Office of Multicultural Initiatives, Student Leadership and Inclusive Excellence, and, most recently, the Dr. Marvin D. Mills, Sr. Multicultural Center.

Tutoring was one of the services at the Minority Student Affairs Office.

Pat Spurgin shows off her Olympic gold medal.

Pat Pitney (née Spurgin) began shooting when she was just nine years old, and it turned out that she had a preternatural talent. She became the first woman to win gold in Olympic rifle shooting in 1984 as an eighteen-year-old freshman at Murray State. She was also selected as the OVC Female Athlete of the Year after becoming the NCAA individual champion in air rifle in 1984, then won the national individual championship in smallbore the following year. In recognition of her many successes as a student athlete at Murray State, Pitney was inducted into the Hall of Fame in 1993 and the campus rifle range was named in her honor. After graduation, she moved to the Last Frontier, where she began coaching the rifle team at the University of Alaska Fairbanks while serving as vice chancellor of admissions. She became president of the University of Alaska system in 2022.

Frank Beamer was named defensive coordinator at Murray State in 1979 after seven seasons as an assistant coach at The Citadel, then he was elevated to head coach in 1981. Beamer was a brilliant innovator, leading Murray State to a 42–23–2 record over his six years as head coach. He introduced a new defensive scheme that helped push the Racers up to the second-ranked rush defense in the country, as well as the fourth-highest scoring defensive unit. The Racers retained a number one rank for six consecutive weeks in I-AA polls, the highest in program history, and Beamer kept the Racers in the top twenty for I-AA teams for twenty-two weeks, the longest streak of its kind. In 1986, Beamer went on to coach at Virginia Tech, leading the Hokies to a remarkable twenty-three consecutive bowl appearances. The term "Beamerball" was coined to reflect on his success utilizing offense, defense, and special teams to score.

Coach Frank Beamer hoisted by his players, including Eric Crigler (68), who became board of regents chair in 2021, after an 1986 win.

Taiwanese Racers represent the International Student Organization at Tent City.

Sheila Smith, the greatest female Racer basketball player of her generation.

Sheila Smith of Memphis was one of the greatest women's basketball players in Murray State history and the first to have her number retired. She starred for the Racers from 1985 to 1989, retiring as the team record holder for points (2,287), points per game (19.7), games played (116), field goals (892), field goal attempts (1,855), three-point field goal attempts (106), free throws made (467), free throw attempts (628), steals (200), and minutes played (3,752). She finished her career as the third-leading scorer in OVC history and was a three-time First Team All-OVC selection at shooting guard. Smith played professionally in France for several seasons after graduation, then became a teacher and basketball coach at Raleigh Egypt High School in Memphis.

Foreign enrollment had grown large enough to form a Foreign Students Organization on campus in 1963, followed in the mid-1980s by the establishment of the International Student Organization, which is now an umbrella for a number of student groups representing different parts of the world. The ISO serves primarily as a support network, a cultural club, a purveyor of great food, and a welcoming meeting place for an increasingly diverse body of students and faculty.

Visitors to the Caribbean might first associate Belize with its beautiful beaches and thriving ecotourism sector, but the country has long been one of the largest sources of foreign students at Murray State thanks to a scholarship program that brings tuition for Belizeans down to near

Murray State education major teaching Belizean students.

the in-state level. The College of Education and Human Services has helped foster the special relationship between Murray State and Belize by sending its education majors on a popular annual three-week in-country teacher training program. Participants broaden their horizons through a life-changing cultural experience, while Belizean students gain a much-anticipated opportunity to learn from American instructors.

| Dr. Jan Weaver, education dean. |

Drs. Jan and Dick Weaver moved to Murray in 1985 with formidable minds and warm hearts. Jan (1931–2009), a dedicated educator originally from Owensboro, joined the College of Education as its dean, while Dick (1927–2018), a former Army Ranger who met her as a student at Indiana University, ran a management consulting firm in the industrial engineering sector after a successful career in aerospace. They were both very active in the community and remained in Murray after their retirements, cheering as loudly as anyone at Racer sporting events. They were frequent and generous donors over the years, particularly in athletics, establishing the Janice F. and Richard F. Weaver Student-Athlete Academic Scholarship and the Dr. Jan Farmer Weaver Endowed Education Scholarship, along with the Weaver Center study space in Stewart Stadium and other legacy gifts that will continue to support Racers for generations to come.

Dr. Stroup's first term coincided with that of Martha Layne Collins, a fellow pioneer who was Kentucky's first and only woman governor from 1983 to 1987. Dr. Stroup and Governor Collins had collaborated to bring a new industry and technology facility to campus, so it was only natural to

| Collins Industry and Technology Center. |

Coach Steve Newton (center) and the 1987–1988 men's basketball team.

name it the Collins Industry and Technology Center when it opened in September 1991. The center houses the Department of Occupational Safety and Health, which prepares students for careers in industry in its laboratories for emergency medical training and industrial hygiene.

The Murray State men's basketball team has qualified for eighteen March Madness tournaments and counting. Their most thrilling run came in 1988, when the Jeff Martin-led Racers took their first-round game against North Carolina State 78–75, then advanced to a second-round match against the formidable University of Kansas squad. The Racers rallied in the second half but came up just short, falling 61–58. The Jayhawks ultimately won the tournament, powering through Xavier, Vanderbilt, Kansas State, Duke, and Oklahoma, but no opponent held them as close as the Racers in that second-round matchup.

The premise of the Student Alumni Association's annual Alumni Weekend Mudball Tournament was simple: have firefighters open their hoses on the intramural field by Hester Hall until they had created six inches of mud, bring in as many teams as possible to play volleyball, and abandon all hope of walking away from it without ending up caked in grime from head to toe. This tradition began in 1989 as a SAA fundraiser and featured some interesting

The Student Alumni Association's annual Alumni Weekend Mudball Tournament.

showdowns, including a 1990 match between the alumni council and the board of regents. When the regents failed to show, the women's volleyball team played in their name and ended up winning the tournament.

Before Mudball, the Alpha Chi chapter of the Sigma Sigma Sigma sorority, aka Tri Sigma, pitted fraternity teams against each other in the more conventional Volley-bash, which was added to Greek Week in 1988. Volleybash ran through the 1990s and featured many fun competitive events capped by a volleyball tournament, with proceeds donated to the Robbie Page Memorial Fund for children with terminal illnesses.

Alumni Relations director Donna Herndon launched Tent City, Murray's biggest and best outdoor party, in the fall of 1989. Every year thousands of Racers past and present come together on the east side of Roy Stewart Stadium between the annual homecoming parade and kickoff at a Racer football game for great food and a variety of fundraising activities sponsored by student and department groups. In recent years, the festivities have grown to nearly fifty tents representing Greek organizations, student clubs, academic departments, and residential colleges.

| Sigma Sigma Sigma's Volleybash. |

| Early Tent City, 1990s. |

Dr. Marvin D. Mills Sr., professor of occupational safety and health.

Eunice Mills rededicates the new Dr. Marvin D. Mills, Sr. Multicultural Center on April 12, 2019.

Dr. Marvin D. Mills Sr. (1921–2018), one of the first Black faculty members at Murray State, was instrumental in the founding and accreditation of the occupational safety and health program. West Virginia-born and Lexington-raised, Mills served in the US Army during the North African and Italian campaigns of World War II and was a postwar military policeman in France. He was awarded many medals for his service, including the French Legion of Honor, the nation's highest merit. After the war, Mills completed a Ed.D. from New York University and embarked on a teaching career that took him to NYU, West Virginia State College, Marshall University, Murray State University, and the University of Cincinnati.

Dr. Mills taught at Murray State from 1977 to 1988, then joined the Murray State University Foundation board in retirement. He tirelessly dedicated himself to ensuring that Black students could succeed at Murray State. The Dr. Marvin D. Mills, Sr. Multicultural Center was named in his honor in 2005. Mills and his wife, Eunice, also established the Dr. Marvin D. Mills Scholarship, which covers tuition, housing, and dining costs for roughly ten Diversity Scholars committed to academic excellence every year. Mills's legacy lives on through the many lives he touched and the significant contributions he made to the university's advancement.

Ronald "Popeye" Jones of nearby Dresden, Tennessee, starred on the hardwood from 1988 to 1992 and went on to play more NBA games than any other Racer. At 6'8" and 250

2018–2019 Mills Emerging Scholars.

pounds, Jones was a high-scoring rebound machine, the only Racer to have put up over 2,000 points and gotten 1,000 rebounds during his college career. In the 1990–1991 season, he was the second-leading rebounder in the country (behind only the legendary Shaquille O'Neal of Louisiana State) and earned OVC Player of the Year honors. The following season, Jones's 14.4 rebounds per game led the nation. Powered by such an impressive individual performance, the Jones-era Racers won four straight regular season OVC championships and went on to three NCAA tournament appearances.

The Houston Rockets selected Jones forty-first overall in the second round of the 1992 NBA draft, and his career took off after a trade to the Dallas Mavericks the following year. Jones played for six teams over eleven solid seasons, averaging 6.9 points and 7.4 rebounds per game before hanging up his sneakers in 2004. Jones transitioned into player development with the Mavericks, then in 2010 he took on NBA coaching duties. He has served as an assistant coach ever since with the New Jersey/Brooklyn Nets, the Indiana Pacers, the Philadelphia 76ers, and, most recently, the Denver Nuggets. Jones passed down his athletic abilities to his sons, Seth and Caleb, but his career took him to a string of hockey-mad cold-weather cities in the late 1990s to early 2000s, so they chose skating over basketball. Both have carved out successful careers as NHL defensemen and were traded separately from their respective organizations to the Chicago Blackhawks in July 2021.

"Popeye" Jones, eleven-year NBA veteran.

Dr. Gene Garfield (1936–2021) was an inspirational professor who joined the political science faculty at Murray State in 1970 while he was completing his Ph.D. at nearby Southern Illinois University. A proud westerner who had lived in Idaho, California, and Utah, he promised his wife it would just be a short stay in Murray before they returned somewhere more familiar, but they fell in love with the community and never left. Garfield's trophy case included awards such as the Max Carmen Outstanding Teacher in 1985, the Alumni Association's Distinguished Professor in 1993, and a Teaching Excellence nod from the regents in 1996.

Dr. Gene Garfield, professor of political science.

Murray State launched its popular semester abroad program in Regensburg, Germany, in 1991.

Heather Samuel, two-time Olympian. Photo courtesy of International Coaching Enrichment Certificate Program.

Kim Koehler-Church, volleyball and track and field star.

Heather Samuel tore up the track from 1991 to 1994 as the greatest female runner Murray State has ever seen. A native of the Caribbean island nation of Antigua and Barbuda, she won the OVC Women's Track Athlete of the Year in 1992, 1993, and 1994. Samuel was a two-time Olympian, competing in the 1992 games in Barcelona and again in Atlanta in 1996. Samuel remains a sporting hero in Antigua and went on to work for its Ministry of Education after retiring from competition.

Racer Hall of Famer Kim Koehler-Church of Marion, Illinois, was an incredibly talented two-sport star from 1987 to 1991. She became the first player in Racer volleyball history to reach 1,000 kills, tied for first with 150 matches played, and ranked second with 528 sets played. Her career highlights included being named MSU Most Valuable Defensive Player her freshman year, three All-OVC First Team selections, three All-Tournament team selections from 1989 to 1991, and an OVC tournament MVP nod. In track and field, Koehler-Church helped lead the Racers to the 1989–1990 OVC indoor championship as well as the OVC outdoor championship in 1991.

Johnny Reagan coached three future major leaguers, the most successful being Kirk "Woody" Rueter, a finesse lefty starter for thirteen seasons between the Montreal Expos and San Francisco Giants. Rueter had doubters at every level and routinely proved them all wrong. College scouts had overlooked him, but his high school American Legion coach in southern Illinois convinced Coach Reagan that Rueter had the talent to succeed against NCAA competition. After a remarkable college career in which he won a Murray State record twenty games from 1989 to 1991 and was named OVC Player of the Year in 1991, Rueter fell all the way to the 477th pick of the MLB amateur draft when he was selected by the Expos. Only around 10 percent of players drafted this late even play in a single major league game, but Rueter rocketed through the Expos system and found himself in the rotation of a very competitive big league club by early July 1993.

Rueter became a fan favorite by using the classic southpaw recipe for success: great command, painting the corners, working quickly, and stellar fielding. That rookie summer he put up eight consecutive wins and was never beaten, pitching to a sterling 2.73 ERA. He was traded to the Giants midseason in 1996 and was a rotation stalwart for a series of great Dusty Baker/Felipe Alou teams through 2005. His greatest individual season came in 1997, when he won thirteen games and put up a 3.45 ERA over 190.2 innings, but he elevated his game even further in eight playoff appearances. The Giants came up just short in a thrilling 2002 World Series against the Anaheim Angels in which Rueter made a quality start in game four and came back

Kirk Rueter, clutch playoff performer. Photo courtesy of the San Francisco Giants.

for a gutsy runless four-inning relief appearance in the decisive game seven. He retired during the 2005 season with 130 career wins and has been curating a massive collection of baseball memorabilia back home in Nashville, Illinois, ever since.

Coach Houston Nutt led the Racers to back-to-back OVC championships in 1995 and 1996, including an absolutely dominant undefeated 11–0 run through regular play in 1995. That team, which included three All-America selections, thumped Western Kentucky in its opening game and beat all challengers other than EKU and Tennessee State by at least twenty-one points. These Racers matched up against Northern Iowa in a first-round Division I-AA playoff game at home on November 25, falling 35–34 after the Panthers blocked an extra point attempt with 1:26 left on the

Coach Houston Nutt motivates his undefeated 1995 football team.

Ginger Adams in 1993–1994 cheering at a Racer basketball game.

clock. This was arguably the greatest Racer football team of all time despite the heartbreaking end to its season.

March Madness is usually a joyous time, but the 1995 tournament was marred by tragedy when the van carrying the Racer cheerleading squad back from Tallahassee on March 17 was hit by a transport truck on I-24 near Cadiz. The truck driver's rear tire blew, causing him to lose control, and the Racer van rolled over multiple times after the collision. All thirteen passengers were hospitalized and twelve recovered. Ginger Adams, a Calloway County High graduate who was an energetic junior co-captain with a 4.0 GPA, died from her injuries a week after the accident. Her teammates pressed through the pain of their loss by competing in her name at the 1996 Universal Cheerleading Association Championship. The university created a scholarship in her memory for education majors and invited her parents, Hafford and Joanna Adams, to accept a BA degree in her honor at graduation in the spring of 1997.

| Springer-Franklin and White residents playing intramural football, 2014. |

Elizabeth College team at an intramural sporting event, 2016.

| Clark and Richmond residents celebrate an impending graduation at All Campus Sing, 2019. |

| 6 |

A New Millennium

1997–2013

Introduction

MURRAY STATE PROGRESSED TOWARD THE CLOSE OF ITS first century with confidence. There was, as always, great men's basketball, highlighted by a pair of pride-inducing March Madness runs in 2010 and again in 2012. Women's athletics expanded in a major second round of growth and counted a number of great triumphs of its own. The university added key infrastructure to provide the Racer community with bigger and better venues for sports, entertainment, and exercise, along with a brand new Paducah regional campus to take high-quality educational opportunities farther afield. Alumni from the arts starred on television and in music, while Murray State's own students began producing their own much appreciated local concert series, Lovett Live! A new slate of joyous, community-building fundraising traditions, Taste of the Arts and the Hutson Harvest Gala, joined the social calendar as well. Above all, however, this was the bright shining moment for a handful of major donors who stepped forward and gave generously at a time when their benevolence was needed most due to declining state appropriations for higher education.

A college or university education opens many doors in life, but a group of alumni who passed through campus in the 1950s and 1960s before going on to enjoy tremendous success in their respective careers thought Murray State had done much more than that. Their experiences here had inspired them, provided a sense of belonging and identity, and shaped their characters for the better. Previous generations of alumni had given back to Murray State in a major way, but this cohort in particular was numerous, open-hearted, and left an enduring legacy across campus. Among them were Dr. Arthur J. Bauernfeind, the Hutson family, Dr. Jesse D. Jones, Dr. Gene W. Ray, and Dr. Jerry and Betsy Shroat, all wonderful benefactors whose contributions will be outlined in due course.

True to our roots, a century after our founding we remain closely tied to the people who make their living on west Kentucky farms, and the school of agriculture is still home to many of our core programs. In the late 1990s and early 2000s, the university took one of its most significant gifts to date, the Pullen Farm, and transformed the property by adding greenhouses and a beautiful Arboretum that showcases the work of the faculty, staff, and students working in horticulture. After twenty years of continuous improvement, there is no more pleasing spot within the city limits in which one can enjoy a leisurely nature walk.

The Hutson family made its name in agricultural supply under patriarch Nicholas Hutson during Murray State's founding era, and the family has provided generous backing ever since. As the business passed through successive generations from Dan Hutson Sr. to Dan Hutson II, the family's support has remained constant. More recently, Cindy and Sue Hutson have continued the giving tradition. Over the years, the Hutsons have funded numerous scholarships, donated a 160-acre laboratory farm, and sponsored the Hutson Harvest Gala in 2014 for supporters of the Arboretum. In 2010, the board of regents paid tribute to their long record of selfless giving by naming the family's dearest campus entity the Hutson School of Agriculture.

In athletics, the opening of the Regional Special Events Center transformed the fan experience at basketball games, offered modern amenities, and expanded seating to accommodate 3,000 more fans than Racer Arena. The later addition of the Gene W. Ray Center for Racer Basketball gave both the men's and women's teams a spacious new practice facility that is the envy of OVC competitors. The 2007–2008 women's team in particular enjoyed its finest season yet, advancing to March Madness on the strong play of star Amber Guffey, who returned to join the coaching staff in 2017. Women's athletics grew in new directions, adding soccer in 2000 and softball in 2008. The soccer team has been wildly successful since its inception, and the softball team showcased the talents of the 2011 OVC Player of the Year, Jenna Bradley, on inviting Racer Field. In individual competition, Morgan Hicks followed in Pat Spurgin's Olympic footsteps, representing Murray State and America in women's rifle at the 2004 Summer Games in Athens. Around the same time, Velvet Milkman, founder of the women's golf program, was leading her players to such great success that she has entered the pantheon as one of the winningest coaches in Murray State history.

In the arts, Racer Nation took enormous pride in the accomplishments of the supremely talented mandolinist and singer Chris Thile, a California kid who relocated to Murray in the 1990s and studied in our music department before fully dedicating himself to a career that has brought him great critical acclaim. Chrishell Stause graduated from the theatre department onto the small

Edward Breathitt's Rainey T. Wells monument was added to the campus quad in 1997.

THE FOUNDER
NEY T. WELLS

Murray State's equestrian team began competition in the late 1990s, giving riders the opportunity to compete in hunt, stock, and dressage.

screen, starring in a number of popular soap operas before transitioning into a Netflix reality series centered around the fast-paced world of high-end Los Angeles real estate. Their triumphs, along with those of their classmates, were proof that Murray State graduates could succeed at the highest levels. The Office of Development created a new fundraiser, Taste of the Arts, to give community members the opportunity to support the next generation of arts majors through live and silent auctions at a delightful formal dinner every October.

Racer Arena was the site of many decades' worth of happy sporting memories, but by the late 1970s it had become too small to accommodate growing crowds of Murray State basketball fans. After years of political deliberations, construction began on a replacement in 1995. The current home

of Racer basketball, the CFSB Center, opened its doors in the fall of 1998. Originally known as the Regional Special Events Center (RSEC), this multipurpose facility has seating for up to 8,600 fans for basketball games and 7,800 for concerts. It took on its current name after the Community Financial Services Bank (CFSB) made a generous donation to Murray State athletics in 2010 during the *Hold Thy Banner High* capital campaign. The first major recording artist to play at the CFSB Cen-

CFSB Center groundbreaking, 1994. Those present included Governor Brereton Jones, Secretary of Transportation Don Kelly, State Senator Jeff Green, Dr. Tim Miller, regents Sid Easley and Jim Butts, Foundation Trustee Harold Doran, and Dr. Bob Jackson (at podium).

A packed house for a game against Belmont on January 24, 2019.

ter was Tim McGraw in September 1998, and over the years Bob Dylan, Nelly, Willie Nelson, Kanye West, and many others have performed there. The CFSB Center also houses the Murray State athletics Burton Family Hall of Champions.

Dr. S. Kern Alexander became the ninth university president in 1994, arriving with a great deal of experience as a higher education administrator and educational advisor to a governor and a future US president. Dr. Alexander

Legendary hoops broadcaster Dick Vitale called the Racers 65–51 victory over Saint Mary's College in a BracketBusters game on February 18, 2012, with a record-setting 8,825 fans in attendance.

President Kern Alexander.

oversaw many changes, including the introduction of the Residential College system, which provided many new opportunities for student life and assisted in enhancing retention efforts. The RSEC was erected, work began on a new science campus, and a new wing–aptly named Alexander Hall–was added to the College of Education and Human Services.

The Zeta Omicron chapter of the Alpha Phi Alpha fraternity began its annual Alpha Step Off fundraiser in 2000 as a creative fundraising outlet to benefit the March of Dimes, a charity that supports the healthcare needs of soon-to-be mothers and babies. The competition, open to both Greeks and non-Greeks, takes place every March at Lovett Auditorium. Stepping is a percussive dance, usually performed in small groups, that has a rich, centuries-long history in the Black community. The first national Greek competitions were held in the 1970s, and it has become increasingly popular in recent decades.

Scott Thile relocated his family in 1995 to take a job at Murray State as a musical instrument technician. His teenage son, Chris, born in Oceanside, California, in 1981, was swaddled in music from an early age and demonstrated enormous talent from the moment he picked up his first instrument. Chris started playing the mandolin at age five and formed his first band, Nickel Creek, a progressive acoustic trio, with Sara and Sean Watkins at age eight. Chris studied music at Murray State in the

Alpha Gamma Delta competes in the Alpha Step Off.

late 1990s with two Nickel Creek albums and a Grammy nomination already under his belt.

Nickel Creek enjoyed critical success on four albums released from 1992 to 2006, but it went on hiatus for seven years as Thile expanded his musical horizons with Punch Brothers, a progressive bluegrass band. Between Nickel Creek and Punch Brothers, Thile has won four Grammy awards along with the BBC's Folk Musician of the Year in 2007 and a pair of trophies from the International Bluegrass Music Association. The ultimate honor came when Thile was awarded the MacArthur Foundation's prestigious Genius Grant in 2012. In 2016, he took over as host for the popular weekly NPR variety radio show *A Prairie Home Companion,* which has since been renamed *Live from Here.* The show features live folk, bluegrass, and roots music, plus comedy skits and interviews.

Draffenville's Chrishell Stause was the standout performer of her generation, a talented Murray State theatre graduate who starred in campus productions as Cecily in *The Importance of Being Earnest* and Shelby in *Steel Magnolias.* She earned her unique portmanteau given name after her mother went into early labor at a Shell station and an attendant named Chris jumped in to help with the delivery. Stause was a regular on several popular daytime soap operas after graduation. She had turns as Amanda Dillon on *All My Children,* Bethany Bryant on *The Young and the Restless,* and Jordan Ridgeway on *Days of Our Lives.* More recently, Stause's work as a high-end realtor has been showcased on Netflix's *Selling Sunset* reality series and she was one of the celebrity competitors in season twenty-nine of *Dancing with the Stars.*

Chrishell Stause on the set of *All My Children.* Photo courtesy of ABC PHOTO ARCHIVES.

Kenyan long-distance runner Wesley Korir won both the 5,000- and 10,000-meter races for Murray State at the 2004 OVC championships. He's pictured here after winning the 2012 Boston Marathon. Photo courtesy of Hyunah Jang/Boston University News Service.

| Morgan Hicks at the 2004 Olympics. |

Morgan Hicks came to Murray State from Tacoma, Washington, in 2000 and became one of the best shooters to ever compete for the rifle team. She racked up eight All-America selections over her career and was the NCAA women's air rifle champion in 2004. Hicks went on to compete for Team USA at the 2004 Summer Olympics in Athens, Greece, finishing twelfth. In 2007 she became head coach for the University of Nebraska-Lincoln rifle program. In 2008 she was a gold medalist in three rifle positions at the International Shooting Sport Federation World Cup.

Dr. Arthur Bauernfeind and his wife, Diana, mark the dedication of the Arthur J. Bauernfeind College of Business in October 2012.

Inside the Susan E. Bauernfeind Student Recreation and Wellness Center.

| Amber Guffey takes it to the hoop for the 2007–2008 women's basketball team. |

The expansive Susan E. Bauernfeind Student Recreation and Wellness Center was dedicated in the spring of 2005 as the most significant campus addition during President F. King Alexander's term. It offers Racers a full range of exercise equipment, an indoor track, three basketball courts, racquet-ball courts, aerobic studios, lap and leisure pools, along with ping pong and billiard tables. Dr. Arthur J. Bauernfeind, a 1960 business graduate and one of Johnny Reagan's baseball players, made a generous donation to help complete the facility, which bears the name of his late daughter. Dr. Bauernfeind had a long and successful career as CEO and chairman of Westfield Capital Management Company in Boston while maintaining his Murray State ties as the former chair of the MSU Foundation Board of Trustees. The university recognized his many years of giving by naming the Arthur J. Bauernfeind College of Business in his honor.

Coach Jody Adams led the 2007–2008 women's basketball team to its greatest season ever. Future Hall of Famer and senior guard Amber Guffey was the team's offensive spark plug, a three point threat and high-proficiency free throw shooter who put up 17.7 points and 4.3 assists per game. These Racers punched their ticket to March Madness after finishing with an overall record of 24–7, running into a very strong no. 3 seeded Duke team that ultimately advanced to the regional semi-finals. After playing professionally in Europe, Guffey rejoined the Racer women's team as an assistant coach.

The Purcell name is synonymous with Murray State athletic excellence thanks to a dynamic father-son duo. Bennie (1929–2016) was a two-time All-OVC pick in basketball who helped lead the Breds to their first ever OVC title in 1951. He was named MVP of the NAIA tournament the following year and became the first Murray State men's basketball player to reach 1,000 career points despite playing in the pre-three point shot era. Bennie toured with the Harlem Globetrotters for a spell and then came back to Murray State in 1963 as assistant men's basketball coach. He became the men's tennis coach in 1969, and his team immediately won an OVC title, the first of eleven they picked up before he turned his whistle over to son Mel after the 1995 season.

Bennie had accumulated eight OVC Tennis Coach of the Year awards and left his son with big shoes to fill, but Mel was a highly accomplished player in his own right who had reached the quarterfinals at Wimbledon in 1983 and had beaten titans of the 1980s tennis world, including Ivan Lendl and Boris Becker. His biggest triumphs as a coach came in 2001 and 2002 when the Racers won back-to-back Ohio Valley Conference championships and competed in the NCAA tournament, leading to two OVC Coach of the Year recognitions. He can be found most days still playing on the campus tennis court that bears his father's name.

Tennis greats Bennie (left) and Mel Purcell.

Executive Director of Development Dr. Tina Bernot bids at Taste of the Arts, 2016.

Taste of the Arts began in October 2009 as a lavish annual fundraiser for Murray State's art, music, and theatre students and has become the most refined evening on the fall social calendar. Over the years Dr. Tina Bernot, the executive director of development, grew the event, which begins with cocktails followed by a silent auction, a fine dinner, and a live auction centered around big ticket experiences, holiday packages, artwork, jewelry, and more.

Everyone who lived through it vividly recalls the ice storm of 2009, one of the region's most disruptive winter weather events in living memory. The freezing rain began during the afternoon of January 26, and power had been knocked out everywhere across the Purchase Area within a day as heavy ice accumulated on and then downed power lines. Compounding matters, a city water main broke, leaving area residents without both electricity and water. Inches of snow and ice blanketed roads, making them nearly impassable, and even basic information was hard to come by after WKMS's regional tower was knocked out.

As local authorities worked around the clock to restore services, the new Murray State police station, just outfitted with a new generator, became Calloway County's command center for relief efforts. Governor Steve Beshear mobilized the National Guard to deal with what he called "the biggest natural disaster in modern Kentucky history" by clearing roads and getting supplies to the worst affected. The university cancelled classes and relocated students to emergency shelters after the water was shut off to prevent pipes from freezing in the residence halls. Many students had to spend the night in Lovett Auditorium, one of the few heated spaces on campus. Despite the cold and hardships, students found a way to make the best of it, venturing outside to go sledding on the hill next to the Curris Center. It took weeks to fully restore power throughout western Kentucky, but Governor Beshear praised Murray State's leading role in supporting the community through the difficult time.

The role of university provost is an incredibly demanding position usually reserved for a well-regarded and highly experienced faculty member. As the senior academic administrator, the pro-

Damage outside Waterfield Library, 2009 ice storm.

The Lovett Live! concert series produced by Racer Live Productions and Murray State's music business students features nationally known performers in a more intimate setting than arena shows at the CFSB Center. Seen here is Holly Williams in 2013.

vost is responsible for curriculum and research. In 2010, Dr. Bonnie Higginson marked another notable women's first at Murray State when she rose to the rank of provost at the culmination of a long and distinguished career in the education department.

Dr. Higginson steadily climbed the ranks at her alma mater, embodying all of the very best characteristics of a Murray State instructor. She graduated from Murray State in 1975 with a Bachelor of Science degree and then again in 1978 with a Master of Science degree in human services. The following year she became the coordinator of the reading and study skills program at Murray State, but she continued her education by pursuing a Ph.D. in reading education from the University of Georgia, which she completed in 1985. It was a rapid rise thereafter to department chair, residential college head, associate provost, and then ultimately provost.

Dr. Higginson was recognized as one of the university's finest instructors on numerous occasions. She was honored with the 1992 Board of Regents Award for Excellence in Teaching and the 2000 Distinguished Professor Award. In 2007 she received the first Murray State University Extraordinary Contribution to Internationalization Award for her leadership in the development of the Belize Inter-

Dr. Bonnie Higginson, provost, 2007.

Dr. Randy Dunn, the eleventh president from 2006 to 2013, married Dr. Ronda Baker at Oakhurst on October 20, 2007.

national Teaching Experience program, among other initiatives. She also received the COEHS Alumni Service Award in 2015. After thirty-three years of service to Murray State, Higginson resigned as provost in 2012 in order to spend her last working years before retirement back in the classroom as a part-time Regents Professor Emeritus. In 2021, Dr. Higginson was honored with the Distinguished Alumni Award by the Murray State Alumni Association.

The 2009–2010 men's basketball team can stake a claim to the best ever in Murray State history, annihilating the OVC with a 17–1 record in conference play and a 31–5 overall mark. The Racers suffered their only OVC loss in a squeaker on the road at Morehead, who they later defeated in the OVC tournament championship game. The Racer offense was powered during the tournament final by freshman guard Isaiah Canaan of Biloxi, Mississippi, who came off the bench to score sixteen points. President Barack Obama, a noted college basketball fan, raised some eyebrows when he picked Murray State to upset Vanderbilt in the first round of his March Madness bracket, but he was ultimately proven correct when Danero Thomas drained a fifteen-foot buzzer beater to give the Racers a thrilling 66–65 victory. In the second round, the Racers went up against the grinding defense of Butler University in another nail-biter. This seesaw affair was tied with just 1:22 to play, then Butler took the lead for good with twenty-five seconds on the clock and shut Canaan down with a double team to secure a 54–52 victory. Racer fans took some solace from their team's gritty performance when Butler advanced all the way to the final.

First-year coach Steve Prohm inherited a powerhouse team when his predecessor, Billy Kennedy, left to take over at Texas A&M, but he somehow managed to lead it to even greater dominance in 2011–2012. This Racer team, with new assistant coach Matt McMahon on the staff, lost only a single regular season game—to Tennessee State, a team they later held off for a 54–52 win in the OVC tournament championship game. Junior Isaiah Canaan had developed into an offensive force as a high-proficiency three-point shooter who put up nineteen points per game, leading the Racers to an overall record of 31–2 as he garnered attention from NBA scouts. The team as a whole rose as high as seventh in the ESPN/USA Today poll rankings and ninth by the Associated Press, setting up a strong bid to become the first OVC team since 1971 to advance to the Sweet Sixteen in March Madness. The Racers manhandled Colorado State 58–41 in a first-round NCAA tourna-

| Isacc Miles goes in for a layup for the 2009–2010 men's basketball team. |

Jewuan Long cuts down the net after the Racers' OVC tournament victory in 2012.

The Office of Development in Heritage Hall coordinates gifts from private donors, who do so much to help sustain the university, its students, and faculty. To learn more, contact msu.giving@murraystate.edu or call (270) 809-3001 or (877) 282-0033.

The Arboretum at Murray State.

ment matchup before facing off against Marquette in the second. They drew to within four points with 7:36 remaining before the Golden Eagles went on a 12–3 run to cinch their victory. In the end, however, this was a truly great team that matched a single season team record for wins.

Stanley Pullen, the first full-time faculty member in the agriculture department back during the normal school days, died young in 1936 and was survived by his widow, Mabel. She then found herself in a bind as she tried to manage their forty-four-acre farm located just north of the current site of Murray High School. Stanley had both a dairy operation, College Crest Farm, and students who needed to learn how farm businesses worked, creating an opportunity for a mutually beneficial collaboration.

Mabel maintained her ties to Murray State's agriculture department, which in turn helped her keep the farm going for many decades. As a symbol of her gratitude, she gifted her entire estate, including the farm, to the agriculture program in her will. The university has since developed the property in a number of ways since acquiring it in 1996. The horticulture division now operates out of Pullen Farm, adding greenhouses and an Arboretum featuring a wide variety of local plants and an events pavilion. The site itself fulfills all sorts of practical needs as an open-air classroom and agronomy testing and research facility, while at the same time serving as the most pleasant outdoor spot in the city.

For local elementary school students, the Hutson School of Agriculture's annual Fall on the Farm competes with Halloween as the most anticipated experience of the season. Agriculture Dean

The Hutson Harvest Gala began in 2014 as a fall fundraiser for the Arboretum. Guests enjoy a fine farm-to-table meal, a performance from local musicians, and both live and silent auctions.

Tony Brannon began this week-long public celebration of all things farm related in 2003 as a means of showcasing his program while giving back to the community and promoting agritourism. The highlights for younger visitors include the barn slide, corn maze, and an opportunity to hold baby chicks. As Fall on the Farm has grown in scope over the years, the Agriculture Leadership Council and the Collegiate Future Farmers of America club have joined in to help manage it.

Murray State offered its first off-campus study centers throughout the Purchase Area back in the 1950–1951 academic year to make its offerings more accessible to a greater number of students. Today, the university operates out of regional campuses on the US Army base at Fort Campbell, at the community colleges in Henderson and Madisonville, and from new state-of-the-art stand-alone Murray State facilities in both Hopkinsville and Paducah.

One of many activities at the School of Agriculture's annual Fall on the Farm event for local students.

Murray State's Paducah regional campus.

Murray State's Alumni Center bears the name of Sid Easley (1940–2016), a Sedalia native and one of the university's biggest boosters. Easley was a born leader who served double duty as both Student Government Association and Pi Kappa Alpha president during his undergraduate years as a political science major. He went on to complete a law degree at UK and served as a captain in the US Air Force from 1965 to 1968, then began a long and successful legal career that included an eight-year run as Calloway County attorney and four years as the First District judge for Calloway and Marshall Counties. Easley was a prolific fundraiser for Murray State who made significant contributions to his alma mater as president of the Alumni Association and the longest-serving chair of the board of regents. He and his wife, Melissa, were major backers of the basketball program, WKMS, and the history department, establishing a major scholarship endowment for Murray State students. In 2014, Easley also proved himself to be a capable true crime writer with the publication of his gripping book *A Courthouse Tragedy: Politics, Murder, and Redemption in a Small Kentucky Town*.

| Sid Easley, air force captain, lawyer, and booster. |

| Dr. Gene W. Ray, scientist, business leader, benefactor. |

Calloway native Gene W. Ray graduated from Murray State with a B.S. in physics, chemistry, and mathematics in 1960 as the Outstanding Senior Man, then continued on to a master's degree in physics followed by a doctorate in theoretical physics at the University of Tennessee before embarking on a highly successful career as a scientist and business leader. In 1981, Dr. Ray founded The Titan Corporation, which broke into the lucrative wireless telecommunications and information technology industries at the dawn of the Internet age. He also served for two years as senior appointee for the US Air Force chief of staff and was charged with leading a team that studied the scientific implications of major national security issues.

Dr. Ray and his wife, Taffin, have always held Murray State close to their hearts, giving generously over the years. One of their biggest gifts helped fund the construction of the Gene W. Ray Center for Racer Basketball connected to the CFSB Center. The Ray Center includes a practice facility, a training center, and office suites for coaches and is used by both the men's and women's teams. Beyond athletics, he has been a major supporter of the Jones College of Science, Engineering and Technology, particularly the Center for Cybersecurity and Network Management, which evolved out of the Telecommunications Systems Management program. As an outstanding alumnus with a giving heart, Dr. Ray was a natural candidate to lend his name to the newly opened Dr. Gene W. Ray Science Campus in 2013.

| Dr. Jerry (center) and Betsy Shroat, theater enthusiasts, at Taste of the Arts. |

Jerry and Betsy Shroat met at Murray State in 1959, forming a deep bond over their shared love of the theatre. Betsy was a Tri Sigma elementary education major from Henderson who performed in Campus Lights, while Jerry was a local training school alumnus turned history/political science major who took to the stage in the senior play and one-man shows. They graduated in 1963, married in 1964, had two children, and built a comfortable life in Ohio. Betsy taught and Jerry rose through the ranks at Progressive Corporation, becoming president of the Personal Lines Division, while both kept busy in various community and charitable endeavors. They reengaged with Murray State in the early 1990s, when Jerry joined the MSU Foundation Board of Trustees and Betsy served on the MSU Library Board. They showed their generous nature with a series of major gifts in the following years. In addition to an endowment, contributions to a capital campaign, and the creation of multiple scholarships, they funded the renovation of the John H. Shroat and James H. Reid Intramural Complex and a new Betsy and Jerry Shroat Stage in the Johnson Theatre. Jerry became chair of the MSU Foundation in 2014.

Velvet Milkman, a stellar twelve-time OVC Coach of the Year and the 2018–2019 interim athletics director, has led the Racer women's golf program since its inception in 1994.

| 7 |

Preparing for a New Racer Century

2013–present

Introduction

THE GREAT RECESSION OF 2008 PROMPTED STATE GOVERNMENTS across the country to make painful cuts to public higher education budgets, but in Kentucky they were some of the deepest and longest-lasting. This forced Murray State, along with all of Kentucky's public universities, to aggressively trim budgets, become more self-reliant, and look to nontraditional sources of funding. Fortunately, a handful of large donors stepped forward once again to help their cherished alma mater through these challenging times.

On January 1, 2013, Murray State entered a new era as it ended its successful fundraising campaign, *Hold Thy Banner High: The Campaign for the Students of Murray State University*. The campaign raised $71.7 million, exceeding the original $60 million goal. Dr. Jesse D. Jones of Baton Rouge, Louisiana, made the lead gift of the campaign with $3.6 million. President Randy Dunn and university leaders invested a great deal of time, travel, and energy during the preceding seven years connecting with alumni and friends to ensure the campaign's success. These efforts significantly increased scholarship endowments, drew in new funds for academic programs, and helped finance campus enhancements.

The *Hold Thy Banner High* campaign was an historic event that resulted in the naming of the first academic units on campus, including the Jesse D. Jones College of Science, Engineering and Technology, the Hutson School of Agriculture, the Bauernfeind College of Business, and the Dr. Gene W. Ray Science Campus. The campaign also funded the naming of the CFSB Center, completed the Charles and Marlene Johnson Lobby in Lovett Auditorium, and brought in gifts for research and laboratory equipment, endowed professorships, athletic programs, buildings, and centers. Donors who gave to the campaign left an indelible mark on nearly every area of the institution, doubling the foundation's privately donated assets and annual scholarship awards.

Coupled with this monumental campaign, our twelfth president, Dr. Tim Miller, brought a familiar and steady hand to the university with his appointment on July 1, 2013, and led legislative efforts during the 2014 General Assembly. Miller along with Dr. Bob Jackson, the Murray State University Foundation president, Dean Steve Cobb, and others secured nearly $32 million from the legislature for the new engineering and physics building, now home to the School of Engineering. This new facility completed the science campus and ensured the growth and enhancement of engineering, engineering technology, physics, and other academic programs. The building was dedicated in 2017 during the tenure of our thirteenth president, Dr. Bob Davies, with many dignitaries in attendance, including Dr. Jesse D. Jones, Lieutenant Governor Jenean Hampton, former presidents, legislators, and members of the board of regents.

In addition, the 2014 General Assembly funded the new Breathitt Veterinary Center in Hopkinsville, a project that our board of regents and several presidents, along with Hutson School of Agriculture Dean Tony Brannon and others, had worked to advance for several years. At the same time, Murray State won approval for the new Hollis C. Franklin Residential Hall, home to the Honors College living and learning community, among other capital projects. The 2014 legislative session resulted in funding and approval for over $100 million of capital construction projects and will be remembered as one of the most successful in our history, preparing Murray State University very well for future growth and expansion.

On August 3, 2018, Dr. Bob Davies notified the board of regents that he would be leaving Murray State University. The board of regents, led by Chair Susan Guess, voted to install Dr. Bob Jackson as the interim president on August 7, 2018, and on March 1, 2019, the board voted to make Jackson the fourteenth president of the university. Dr. Jackson had a long history with Murray State and had held volunteer and administrative roles dating back to his time as a student. Dr. Jackson, a 1985 graduate, was a unique choice in this role as an alumnus, native Kentuckian, and former state legislator; his wife, Karen, is also an alumna.

Dr. Jackson had served as the president of the Murray State University Foundation from 2013 through his appointment as interim president in 2018. He was succeeded at that time by Dr. David Durr, a distinguished finance professor. Jackson was a Golden Horseshoe recipient who had served in other roles as the university's chief development officer, director of the *Hold Thy Banner High* fundraising campaign, Alumni Association president, and state senator representing the First Senatorial District.

Graduating students pause to take a selfie at the spring 2021 commencement ceremony.

During the fall of 2018, Dr. Jackson discussed his vision as we planned our next century with a renewed focus on student recruiting and retention, adding new scholarship programs and need-based initiatives for students, providing academic enhancements, creating a new strategic plan, and funding campus improvements, coupled with the development of a new student housing plan.

However, our institutional vision and plans were interrupted in March 2020 as the COVID-19 pandemic gripped the world, causing Murray State to alter all campus operations. This period was one of the most challenging times in our history as it impacted finances, disrupted classroom instruction, and prompted the implementation of unfamiliar campus safety and healthcare protocols. The addition of a COVID-19 vaccination clinic located in the CFSB Center allowed healthcare professionals to administer 11,000 vaccinations in early 2021.

Most importantly, the administration had to ensure the health and safety of students, faculty, and staff while continuing campus operations during this period of near-daily pandemic disruptions. For many, this was a time of around-the-clock work to address the ever-changing health and safety guidance from the state and federal governments and healthcare professionals. The pandemic began to wane during early 2021, but a wave of late summer infections from a new, more contagious strain of the virus derailed plans for a return to normal in the fall semester.

The June 4, 2021, board of regents meeting was one of the most productive in recent history. The board, led by Chair Jerry Rhoads, approved a new budget coupled with a $12.3 million campus improvement plan to benefit academic programs, campus and student activities, and other major initiatives. These funds and those already designated will be used to renovate Lovett Auditorium, make improvements to our historic buildings, provide other infrastructure needs, and ensure enhancements and a modernization plan for the Curris Center. This was a major step in addressing many initiatives on campus and to prepare Murray State for its centennial celebration in 2022.

Finally, Murray State University, like all institutions of higher learning, has a unique and important history. This institution has touched the lives of tens of thousands of individuals. During the past 100 years, we have responded to many challenges and opportunities, and each has been addressed by excellent leadership from our board of regents, presidents, administrators, faculty, staff, students, and our alumni and friends. These individuals left a lasting mark and a path forward for the next generation. Our founder, Dr. Rainey T. Wells, and first president, Dr. John W. Carr, along with members of the early boards of regents who had the vision, perseverance, and courage to imagine this special place, would be very proud of where we have arrived today. As always, our best days are ahead of us.

Dr. Tim Miller spent over forty years on campus as a beloved faculty member, former chair of the Department of Accounting, executive director of the Murray State University Foundation, proud alumnus, and twelfth president in 2013–2014. Dr. Miller was a highly competent administrator and a first-rate instructor who accumulated numerous teaching awards over the decades. On his retirement in 2014, the new Dr. Tim Miller Center for Accounting Education was dedicated in his honor as a state-of-the-art business facility for Murray State students.

Dr. Tim Miller, daughter Anne (left), and wife Patsy, at the unveiling of his official portrait in the Department of Accounting in 2018.

Jim Carter, longtime vice president of institutional advancement and executive director of the Alumni Association, was a big thinker with a special skill for connecting with alumni and friends. He oversaw many campus and alumni activities during his twenty-seven-year tenure at Murray State. The university lost one of its finest when he lost a battle with cancer in 2015 at the age of fifty-seven. The Alumni Plaza is named in his honor.

The first major gift of the *Hold Thy Banner High* campaign came from Dr. Jesse D. Jones of Baton Rouge, Louisiana, to build the Jesse L. Jones Family Clock Tower, a campus landmark. Jones unlocked his potential at Murray State in the early 1960s as a nontraditional student from Marshall

Jim Carter, longtime vice president and alumni director.

Jesse L. Jones (center), and his family, break ground for the new clock tower that bears his name.

County, completing a B.S. in chemistry and mathematics as a married father with two children and a night shift job at a Calvert City plant. After graduation, Jones relocated to Baton Rouge to work in turn as a successful plastics engineer, project manager, and sales leader for the Ethyl and later Albemarle Corporations. Over the years his work contributed to nineteen patents and his business took him all over the world. Thanks to his ongoing support of the university, the Jesse D. Jones Chemistry Building and Jones College of Science, Engineering and Technology bear his name, along with other centers, professorships, and campus initiatives.

Dr. Bob Jackson ('85) and his wife, Karen ('84), are proud alumni, longtime supporters, and have been on campus as students, volunteers, student group advisors, administrators, and in their current roles for over forty years. Prior to his appointment as the fourteenth president, Dr. Jackson had

Dr. Jesse D. Jones, his wife Deb, their family, and former Board of Regents Chair Alan Stout (left) dedicate the Jesse L. Jones Family Clock Tower with the Racer community in October 2007.

Alpha Sigma Alpha members on the last day of sorority recruitment in front of the Jesse L. Jones Family Clock Tower on the Dr. Gene W. Ray Science Campus, August 23, 2021.

| New laboratories and research equipment provide numerous opportunities for our students and faculty. |

served as the university's chief development officer, director of the *Hold Thy Banner High* fundraising campaign, Alumni Association president, state senator, and president of the Murray State University Foundation.

David Dill served as one of the national co-chairs of the *Hold Thy Banner High* campaign and is a trustee of the Murray State University Foundation. He and his wife, Ashley, both alumni and longtime supporters, made a generous gift to create the David and Ashley Dill Distinguished Professorship in Accounting to assist the department with enhanced teaching and research opportunities. David is the president and chief executive officer of a national healthcare company based in Brentwood, Tennessee. He was selected as a 2015 Distinguished Alumnus of Murray State.

Alumni Dr. Melvin and Rita Henley have been cornerstones of Murray State for decades. Dr. Henley is a US Air Force veteran who taught in and chaired the chemistry department, later serving as a state representative, mayor, and city council member in addition to holding many leadership

President Bob Jackson (left) and Dan Kemp, former chair of the board of regents.

Ashley and David Dill, benefactors.

Alumni Dr. Gary W. Boggess (left) and Dr. Jesse D. Jones, friends and one-time high school basketball rivals, at the dedication of the Boggess Science Resource Center in 2017. Dr. Boggess (1936–2017) came back to Murray State as a chemistry professor, then served as dean of science from 1978 until his retirement in 1998.

positions at the university. Dr. Henley, a lifelong resident of Calloway County, holds a unique place in MSU history after having met every Murray State president from Dr. John W. Carr to Dr. Bob Jackson.

College-bound students from Hopkins County have had no bigger boosters than Madisonville's Badgett family. J. Rogers Badgett (1917–2005) was an Arkansas-born and Memphis-raised business owner who opened his first mines during World War II, extracting bauxite in Missouri and then coal in Hopkins and Muhlenberg Counties. In

Dr. Melvin Henley and his wife, Rita, homecoming grand marshals in 2018.

Senior engineering students with their E-Vehicle project, 2021.

| The Hutsons have been major supporters since the founding era. |

Charles Edward Hall, a 1973 theatre graduate and the longest-serving Radio City Music Hall Santa.

Radio City Music Hall.
Photo Courtesy of William Warby.

time, he became a construction, energy, and transportation magnate with an international reach as well as a minority owner of the Boston Red Sox from 1978 to 1985. The J. Rogers Badgett Foundation serves as the family's philanthropic vehicle and has become a generous source of scholarships for Hopkins County students, enabling them to participate in the 2+2 program, beginning their programs at Madisonville Community College, then transferring to Murray State. Another major foundation initiative provides teachers with scholarships to pursue master's degrees at Murray State's regional campus in Madisonville. Over 400 Racers and counting have benefitted from more than $1.1 million worth of Badgett scholarships since their inception in 2009. Bentley Badgett, president, and his daughter, Rhea Ashby, vice president, manage the foundation's philanthropic efforts.

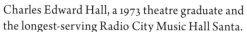

Murray State opened the new Engineering and Physics Building in October 2017, followed by the August 2020 launch of the School of Engineering, as part of a continued effort to support and grow engineering, engineering technology, and physics, among other academic programs. The School of Engineering, led by Dr. Danny Claiborne, offers hands-on learning opportunities in exciting, high-

Bentley Badgett and Rhea Ashby, MSU Foundation trustee, at the Madisonville Community College Gala.

Preparing for a New Racer Century | 139

Engineering student Clay Doran manufactures desperately needed personal protective equipment in the Engineering and Physics Building during the early days of the COVID-19 pandemic.

growth fields along its mechanical, electrical, and aerospace tracks, in part by deepening collaboration with area businesses. Dr. Claiborne's team demonstrated some of the school's more practical applications in the spring of 2020 when it began 3D-printing desperately needed plastic visors for medical professionals at Murray-Calloway County Hospital and beyond during the early days of the COVID-19 pandemic.

Star guard and Racer Hall of Famer Cameron Payne out of Memphis had two great seasons in blue and gold before the Oklahoma City Thunder selected him fourteenth overall in the 2015 NBA draft. A series of injuries hampered his development with the Thunder and then the Chicago Bulls, but everything came together for him after signing with the Phoenix Suns in June 2020. Payne elevated his game in the spring of 2021, highlighted by a nineteen-point and seven-assist night against fellow Racer alumnus Ja Morant and the Memphis Grizzlies on February 20. Payne was especially strong in the playoffs as the Suns powered through to the NBA finals for the first time since 1993.

Murray State's women's soccer program was founded in 2000 and is still a relative newcomer to the campus sports scene, but the team has been in full-throttle dynasty mode since 2015. These Racers picked up their first OVC championship in 2008, winning the tournament again in 2015, 2017, and 2018, then reaching the semifinals in both 2019 and 2020. All of this winning led to three NCAA tournament appearances. Aussie import Harriet Withers starred for the 2014–2017 Racer teams as an explosive scorer who racked up thirty-eight goals over seventy-seven games en route to enshrinement in the Racer Hall of Fame.

Cameron Payne with the Phoenix Suns against the Los Angeles Clippers. Photo courtesy of NBAE Getty Images.

Soccer star Harriet Withers celebrates one of her thirty-eight career goals.
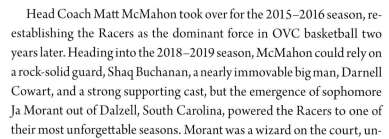

Head Coach Matt McMahon took over for the 2015–2016 season, reestablishing the Racers as the dominant force in OVC basketball two years later. Heading into the 2018–2019 season, McMahon could rely on a rock-solid guard, Shaq Buchanan, a nearly immovable big man, Darnell Cowart, and a strong supporting cast, but the emergence of sophomore Ja Morant out of Dalzell, South Carolina, powered the Racers to one of their most unforgettable seasons. Morant was a wizard on the court, unlike any player Racer fans had ever seen. Over the course of the year, he had fifteen games with over twenty points and ten assists when no other college player in the country had more than three. His electrifying play elevated everyone around him. The Racers charged into the OVC tournament after a 28–5 season, fending off a veteran Jacksonville State team in the semifinals before handily beating their greatest rival, Belmont, in the final to earn an automatic March Madness berth. The NCAA tournament began with a bang in the form of a nineteen-point victory over Marquette before the Racers were overmatched by Florida State in the Round of 32.

Many teams have great players, but few have stars so bright that they are universally known by their first name alone. To the Racer faithful, Ja is that player. He debuted as a point guard for the Racers in the fall of 2017 and made an immediate impact, earning First Team All-Conference honors as a freshman. His collegiate career highlights included a First Team All-America selection after his sophomore year, an OVC Player of the Year Award, and the distinction of leading the NCAA in assists in 2018–2019. Under the guidance of Coach McMahon, the 2018–2019 Morant-led Rac-

OVC competitors could not contain the Ja Morant-led 2018–2019 Racers. Pictured left to right: Tevin Brown (10), Darnell Cowart (32), Shaq Buchanan (11), and Morant (12).

ers will be remembered as one of the best in university history. Murray State retired Morant's number 12 jersey on February 1, 2020.

Morant forged an alliance between Racer Nation and Grizzlies Nation after Memphis drafted him second overall, the highest ever pick for a Murray State player, in the 2019 NBA Draft. The only remaining question was just how great he would become as a professional. He followed his 2019–2020 rookie of the year season at just age twenty with even better results in his sophomore effort, averaging 19.1 points and 7.4 assists per game, leading the Grizzlies to their first play-off appearance since 2017. He also became only the fourth player in NBA history to score 100-plus points across his first three postseason games, cementing his status as one of the best young point guards in the league.

Racer Nation shows its love for Ja during the Memphis Grizzlies' Murray State night on January 17, 2020.

Susan Guess (left), former board chair and senior vice president of marketing at Paducah Bank, and Jeanie Morgan (right), advisor to student organizations for over forty years.

On December 3, 2018, Dr. Bob and Karen Jackson commemorated Oakhurst's 100th anniversary with a reception. In 2019, First Lady Karen Jackson oversaw the restoration of the historic home's original 1918 oak hardwood floors.

Provost Tim Todd (right) and Board of Regents Vice Chair Dr. Don Tharpe (left) share a laugh.

Students participating in an Esports competition, February 26, 2021.

The beloved Racer Band grew bigger and better than ever under longtime assistant director of bands John Fannin, who retired in 2020 after twenty-five years at Murray State.

On February 13, 2020, retired US Navy four-star admiral William H. McRaven delivered a riveting keynote address at the 2020 Presidential Lecture in Lovett Auditorium. Admiral McRaven holds a unique tie to Murray State University through his father, Colonel Claude "Mac" McRaven, a 1939 graduate, Murray State Hall of Fame football player and track star, and later a World War II fighter pilot. Admiral McRaven gained international renown through his command of the special forces that captured deposed Iraqi dictator Saddam Hussein and rescued Captain Richard Phillips from Somali pirates. He oversaw the mission to capture 9/11 mastermind Osama bin Laden in 2011 and is a former chancellor of the University of Texas system.

During his lecture, McRaven recalled, "growing up, my father used to talk about Murray State like it was hallowed ground.... I talk about my father quite a bit because I like to think what my father learned here at Murray State was so much more than just athletics. He was a remarkable athlete; he had those skills when he got here, but I will tell you what Murray State taught him was how to be a man. The lessons that he took away, he passed on to me."

Admiral Bill McRaven at Lovett Auditorium, February 13, 2020.

In April 2021, the Department of Music hosted the first concert on the site of the future Woods Park, a new green space being developed at the corner of North 14th and Olive Streets.

The Racer One statue on the north side of the Curris Center was dedicated at Homecoming 2020. Dr. Jack and Janice Rose provided the lead gift. Additional donors included Dick and Maureen Anderson, David and Ashley Dill, Frank and Susan Doran, Harold and Kelly Doran, Dr. Melvin and Rita Henley, Dr. Michael and Lana Porter, Kris and Lori Robbins, Dennis and June Smith, and the Friends of Pinnacle.

Former education professor, dean, school superintendent, and mayor Dr. Jack Rose (1943–2020) and his wife, Janice, made the lead gift to fund one of the newest campus landmarks, the Dr. Carr monument added in front of John W. Carr Hall in the fall of 2020.

Football is supposed to be a fall sport, but thanks to COVID-19 the 2020 Racer football season had an unusually late February 28, 2021, kickoff. The Racers got off to a fast start, winning their first five games before finishing 5–2. It was a challenging, abbreviated season for everyone trying to make a contact sport work during a time of strict COVID mitigation protocols, but the on-field results were better than at any point since the late 1990s and auger well for the near future.

Murray State added Kevin Saal (left) as its athletics director and Dean Hood (right) as its football coach in 2019.

The 2021 Racer football team.

Golden Horseshoe recipients and supporters of the arts, Dr. Charles and Marlene Johnson. The Johnsons were Campus Lights performers in the mid-1950s and then became lifelong educators. They presided over the dedication of the Charles and Marlene Johnson Lobby at Lovett Auditorium on December 5, 2019.

2021–2022 freshmen enjoying activities at the Great Beginnings Racer Life event to welcome incoming students to campus.

Regents approved the university's largest ever bond for maintenance and asset preservation in June 2021. Board Chair Jerry Rhoads is pictured beneath the projector screen, and to his left is Senior Administrator Jill Hunt. Alumnus Phil Schooley, far left, the longest-serving staff regent in our history, passed away unexpectedly on August 15, 2021.

| The Rainey T. Wells statue modeling good pandemic behavior. |

The university began preparing for an unprecedented and world-crippling health crisis in February 2020, appointing Jordan Smith as the university's COVID-19 officer. For over a year, there were near-daily pivots regarding health guidance, mask mandates, testing and cleaning protocols, and alterations to every component of campus life. Students, faculty, staff, and administrators all made major sacrifices in order to keep each other safe as online teaching, remote work, and Zoom sessions replaced traditional methods of conducting university business.

Smith, Nursing Dean Dina Byers, along with our faculty in the School of Nursing and Health Professions, and over 125 student nurses and students from other departments assisted in our regional vaccination clinic held at the CFSB Center from February 14 through May 7, 2021, giving over 11,000 vaccinations. In addition, Vice Presidents Jackie Dudley and Don Robertson, Provost Tim Todd, Dr. Bob Hughes, Chief of Police Jeff Gentry, Karen Jackson, the Murray-Calloway County Health Department, the Murray-Calloway County Hospital, and many others provided health and safety assistance throughout the pandemic. This highly effective partnership helped grind local transmission of the third wave of this deadly disease to a near halt by the middle of March 2021, offering a temporary midsummer reprieve before the Delta variant brought a fourth wave in late July.

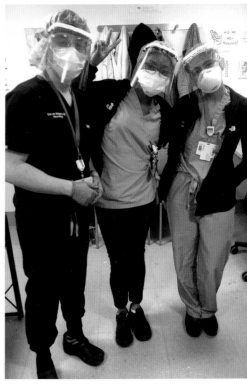

Above: Simple and ubiquitous, face masks saved many lives.

Right: Critical care doctors and staff at New York Presbyterian Hospital, the heart of the US coronavirus epidemic in early 2020, wearing face shields donated by Murray State's School of Engineering.

CFSB vaccination center volunteers ready to administer shots.

Students at the May 8, 2021, commencement ceremony.

The Jesse L. Jones Family Clock Tower on the Dr. Gene W. Ray Science Campus at sunset, lit green in solidarity with those who lost loved ones to COVID-19.

Epilogue

T HE OVC POLLS ITS MEN'S BASKETBALL COACHES EVERY October on their expectations for the upcoming season. In 2021, there was a general consensus that Belmont would take the conference, Morehead would finish a strong second, and Murray State would lag behind as coach Matt McMahon looked to integrate transfers Carter Collins and Trae Hannibal into a squad led by fourth-year stars Tevin Brown and K. J. Williams. OVC coaches were not wrong about Belmont and Morehead, both excellent teams that had strong seasons, but they did badly underestimate the group Coach McMahon had put together.

The Racers were undefeated (18–0) in conference play for just the second time in their history and took a 20-game winning streak, the longest in the country, into March Madness on the heels of a dominant 30–2 season. Their first-round matchup against the University of San Francisco was an overtime thriller, but the Racers fell short in their second tournament contest against a plucky St. Peter's team that had just knocked off the heavily favored University of Kentucky. Regardless, the general postseason consensus in Racer Nation is that fans had just witnessed one of the greatest Murray State teams ever to take the court and that McMahon, who began a new journey at Louisiana State in the spring of 2022, was one of our finest and most inspirational coaches.

Following McMahon's departure, the university selected a former head coach at Murray State and Iowa State, Steve Prohm, for a second tour of duty. He had been an assistant under Billy Kennedy and became the head coach in 2011, leading the Racers to a 104–29 record, two OVC championships, and a 2012 NCAA tournament win over Colorado State over four seasons. Coach Prohm's teams were incredibly tough on the OVC, losing just 10 conference games.

Every new undergraduate can relate to the bittersweet feeling of leaving a comfortable home behind to take on a new challenge born of growth and maturity. The end of the 2021–2022 athletics season brought a momentous change as Murray State left the OVC after seventy-four years to join the Missouri Valley Conference. This historic move was largely motivated by a desire to give Murray State's student athletes the opportunity to compete at an even higher level as the university begins its second century. The coming years will bring new rivals and see the creation of fresh legends, but the true Murray State values of spirit and community will continue to define us just as they have ever since our founding in 1922.

Above: DaQuan Smith scores against the University of San Francisco in a first-round game of the 2022 NCAA men's basketball tournament.

Left: Coach McMahon confers with Trae Hannibal (2), Tevin Brown (10), and Justice "Juice" Hill (14) during a home game against the University of Tennessee at Chattanooga on December 18, 2021.

Appendix

Murray State University Leadership

Murray State University Presidential Administrations

Dr. John W. Carr (1923–1926, 1st term) (1933–1936, 2nd term)

Dr. Rainey T. Wells (1926–1932)

Dr. James H. Richmond (1936–1945)

Dr. Ralph H. Woods (1945–1968)

Dr. M. O. Wrather (1968), Acting President

Dr. Harry M. Sparks (1968–1973)

Dr. Constantine W. Curris (1973–1983)

Dr. Kala M. Stroup (1983–1989)

Dr. James L. Booth (1989–1990), Acting President

Dr. Ronald J. Kurth (1990–1994)

Dr. S. Kern Alexander (1994–2001) (2006, Interim Term)

Dr. F. King Alexander (2001–2005)

Dr. Randy J. Dunn (2006–2013)

Dr. Thomas I. Miller (2013–2014) (2006, Interim Term)

Dr. Robert O. Davies (2014–2018)

Dr. Robert L Jackson (2018–present)

President's Executive Council, 2022

Jackie Dudley, *Vice President for Finance and Administrative Services*

Camisha Pierce Duffy, *Executive Director of Institutional Diversity, Equity and Access and Title IX Coordinator*

Dr. Renee Fister, *Executive Director of Strategic Enrollment Management*

Courtney Hixon, *Director of Human Resources*

Jill Hunt, *Senior Executive Coordinator for the President, Coordinator for Board Relations and Secretary to the Board*

Dr. Bob Jackson, *President*

Rob Miller, *General Counsel*

Dr. Bob Pervine, *Associate Provost*

Dr. Don Robertson, *Vice President for Student Affairs and Enrollment Management*

Kevin Saal, *Director of Athletics*

Jordan Smith, *Executive Director for Governmental and Institutional Relations*

Dr. Timothy S. Todd, *Provost and Vice President for Academic Affairs*

Shawn Touney, *Executive Director of Marketing and Communication*

Murray State University Deans, 2022

Dr. David Eaton, *Dean, Arthur J. Bauernfeind College of Business*

Dr. David Whaley, *Dean, College of Education and Human Services*

David Balthrop, *Dean, College of Humanities and Fine Arts*

Dr. Claire Fuller, *Dean, Jesse D. Jones College of Science, Engineering and Technology*

Dr. Tony Brannon, *Dean, Hutson School of Agriculture*

Dr. Dina Byers, *Dean, School of Nursing and Health Professions*

Cris Ferguson, *Dean of University Libraries*

Centennial Book Committee

Cris Ferguson (Co-Chair), *Interim Dean of University Libraries*

Jordan Smith (Co-Chair), *Executive Director for Governmental and Institutional Relations*

Dr. Tina Bernot, *Executive Director of Development*

Jackie Dudley, *Vice President for Finance and Administrative Services*

Cami Duffy, *Executive Director of Institutional Diversity, Equity and Access and Title IX Coordinator*

Jill Hunt, *Senior Executive Coordinator for the President, Coordinator for Board Relations and Secretary to the Board*

Ashley Ireland, *Interim Associate Provost and Director of Online Programs*

Minae "Mia" Ishijima, *Murray State Student*

Dr. Robert L Jackson, *President*

Chelsea Jones, *Murray State Student*

Molly Logsdon, *Murray State Student*

Carrie McGinnis, *Director of Alumni Relations*

Dr. Sean J. McLaughlin, *Associate Professor, University Libraries and Director of Special Collections and Exhibits*

Kim Newbern, *Coordinator for Greek Life and Student Leadership Programs*

Sarah Marie Owens, *Library Specialist*

Shawn Reynolds, *Member, Board of Trustees and Former President Murray State University Alumni Association*

Dr. Don Robertson, *Vice President for Student Affairs and Enrollment Management*

Darren Russell, *Murray State Student*

Dr. Tim Todd, *Provost and Vice President for Academic Affairs*

Shawn Touney, *Executive Director of Marketing and Communication*

Dave Winder, *Associate Athletic Director, Communication and Public Relations*

Back row, from left: Shawn Reynolds, Cami Duffy, and Dave Winder. Middle row: Carrie McGinnis, Tina Bernot, Jill Hunt, Jackie Dudley, Shawn Touney, Ashley Ireland, and Tim Todd. Seated: Jordan Smith, Sean McLaughlin, Robert Jackson, Sarah Owens, and Cris Ferguson.

Index

Page numbers in italics refer to illustrations

ACS. *See* All Campus Sing
Adams, Ginger, 86, *86*
Adams, Jody, 104
African American Student Service and Ethnic
    Programs, 77
Agriculture Leadership Council, 115
Alexander, Kern, x, 72, 96, 98, *98*, 104
Alexander Hall, 98
All Campus Sing (ACS), 43, 51, *51*, 75, *89*
Allen, James Lane, 11
Allenian Society (A.C.E.), 11, *12*
Allison, Carrie, *24*, 25
Alpha Chi, 81
Alpha Gamma Delta, 73, *73*
Alpha Gamma Rho, 55, 57, *57*
Alpha Omega, 57
Alpha Phi Alpha, 76, *76*, 98
Alpha Sigma Alpha, 75, *130*
Alpha Step Off, 98, *98*
Alpha Tau Omega, *67*, 67–68
alumni: in the arts, 34, 90; giving by, 91 (*see
    also* donors); at Homecoming, *22*; military
    veterans, 29–30, 36; number of, x. *See also
    individual alumni*
Alumni Association, 11
Alumni Weekend Mudball Tournament, *80*, 80–81
American Athletic Conference, 48
Anderson, Dick and Maureen, *150*
Apollo missions, 45
Applied Sciences and Technology, 43
Arboretum, 91, 114, *114–15*
Arnold, Geneva, 43

Arthur J. Bauernfeind College of Business, *102*,
    104, 123
Arts and Sciences, 43
Ashby, Rhea, 138, *139*
athletics. *See specific sports and* women's athletics
Austin, A. B., xi

Badgett, Bentley, 138, *139*
Badgett, J. Rogers, 134, 138
Banks, Marshall, 49
baseball, 46, 48, 52, *66*, 66–67, 71. *See also
    individual players*
basketball: arenas/homes for, 14, 21, 46, *46*,
    55, 94; Black players recruited for, 50, *50*;
    under Hodges, *45*; Marine Corps, 39; under
    McMahon, 142–43; men's, 31, *31*, 80, *80*;
    under Newton, *80*; under Prohm, 108, 114;
    women's (*see* women's athletics, basketball).
    See also individual players
Bauernfeind, Arthur J., 91, *102*, 104
Bauernfeind, Diana, *102*
Beamer, Frank, 77, *77*
Belize International Teaching Experience program,
    72, *78*, 78–79, 107–8
Bernot, Tina, 106, *106*
Beshear, Steve, 106
Beta Nu, 75
Betsy and Jerry Shroat Stage, 121
Big Apple Cafe, 64, *64*
bin Laden, Osama, 149
Birdsong, Eff Weeks, Jr., *61*, 61–62
Black Advisory Council, 59, *59*

Blackburn, Walter, 19, *19*
Blackburn Science Building, 19
Black Student Union, 59
Blondet, Hector, *50*
Boeing Company, 45
Boggess, Gary W., *134*
Boggess Science Resource Center, *134*
Booker, David, *32*
Bradley, Jenna, 91
Brandon, Bobby Leonard, 43
Brannon, Tony, 114–15, 123
Breathitt Veterinary Center (Hopkinsville, Ky.), 71,
    74, 74–75, 123
Brooks, Ernest T., 59, *59*
Brown, Tevin, *143*
Brown, W. Earl, 71, 76, *76*
Brown v. Board of Education, 43, 48
Buchanan, Shaq, 142, *143*
Buckingham, David, *65*
Bumphus, Walter, 55, 60, *60*, 76
Burton, Paula, 51
Burton, Robert G., Sr., 50–51, *51*
Burton Family Hall of Champions, 51, 96
Business, College of, 43–45
Butts, Jim, *95*
Byers, Dina, 155

Calloway County (Kentucky), 2–3, *4*, 6
Calloway Normal School (Kirksey, Ky.), 6
Campus Lights, 32, *32*, 120, *154*
Canaan, Isaiah, 108
Carlisle Cutchin Stadium, *24*, 24–25, 29
Carman, Max, 19, *19*
Carr, John W., x, *7*, *10*; background of, 7; influence
    of, 126; as Murray State Normal School
    president, 4, 6–8; as a teacher, 7; visionary
    statement by, xi
Carroll, Julian, 74
Carter, Jim, 127, *127*
Carter, John Mack, 47, *47*
Caudill, William, 9
Center for Cybersecurity and Network
    Management, 119
CFSB Center (*formerly* Regional Special Events
    Center), 46, 91, 95, *96*, 123, 155
Cherry Expo Center (*formerly* West Kentucky
    Livestock and Exposition Center), 67, *67*
Chicago Bears, *34*, 35
Chicago Seven, 63
Civilian Pilot Training Program, 29
civil rights movement, 58–59
Claiborne, Danny, 138, 140
Clara Eagle Art Gallery, 61, *61*

Clark, Lee, *8*, 8–9
Clark Hall, 9
Cleveland, Grover, 18
Clinton College (Hickman County, Ky.), 2
Cobb, Steve, 123
Coffey, Carla, 56–57, *57*
Cold War, 61
Cole, Ruth E., 44, *44*
College Bulletin, 35
College Crest Farm, 114
College News (later *Murray State News*), 11, 14, *14*
College of Education and Human Services, 79, *79*,
    98
College of Industry and Technology, 41
Collegiate Future Farmers of America, 115
Collins, Martha Layne, 79–80
Collins Industry and Technology Center, 71, 73,
    79, 79–80
Community Financial Services Bank, 95. *See also*
    CFSB Center
computers, 70–71
counterculture (1960s), 62
COVID-19 pandemic, 126, 140, *140*, 152, 155,
    156, *158*
Cowart, Darnell, 142, *143*
Crigler, Eric, 77
Cunningham, Bill, 53, *53*
Curris, Constantine ("Deno"), *64*, 64–65, 73
Curris, Elena Diane, *64*, 65
Curris Center, 54–55, 68, *69*
Curtis, Mike, 62
Cutchin, Carlisle, 24, 31, *31*

dances, *27*
Danielson, Robert, *64*
Davies, Bob, 123
Day Law, 43
Demartra, Nancy Tyler, 48, *49*, 50
Democratic National Convention (1968), 63
Dennis Jackson Racer Room, 49
Department of Music, 149
Department of Occupational Safety and Health, 80
Derby Week, 55, 57, *57*
desegregation, 43, 48–50
Dill, David and Ashley, 132, *133*, *150*
donors, *112*, 118–19, *150*. See also *Hold Thy Banner*
    High campaign
Doran, Clay, *140*
Doran, Frank and Susan, *150*
Doran, Harold, *95*, *150*
Doran, Kelly, *150*
Doyle, Price ("Pop"), *33*, 33–34
Dr. Carr monument, *152*

Dr. Gene W. Ray Science Campus, 119, 123, *130*, *158*

Dr. Jan Farmer Weaver Endowed Education Scholarship, 79

Dr. Marvin D. Mills, Sr. Multicultural Center, 77, 82, *82*

Dr. Marvin D. Mills Scholarship, 82

Dr. Tim Miller Center for Accounting Education, 126

Dudley, Jackie, 155

Dunker mascot, 55, *67*

Dunn, Randy, *108*, 122–23

Dunn, Ronda Baker, *108*

Durr, David, 123

Eagle, Clara M., 61

Earhart, Amelia, 37

Easley, Melissa, 118

Easley, Sid, *95*, 118, *118*

Eastern Kentucky State Normal School No. 1 (Richmond, Ky.), 3

Education, College of, 43

Education Amendments Act (1972), 56

Edwards, Linda, *55*

Eisenhower, Dwight D., 38

Ellis, Holmes, 63

Engineering, School of, 123, 138, 140, *156*

Engineering and Physics Building, 138, *140*

Epsilon Lambda, 75

Epsilon Tau, 57

equestrian team, *94*

Esports, *147*

E-Vehicle project, *135*

Faculty Senate, 54

Fall on the Farm, 114–15, *115*

Fannin, John, *148*

Federal Communications Commission, 59

Federal Works Administration, 41

Fifty Years of Progress (Woods), x

fine arts, 33–34

First National Bank, *5*

football: under Beamer, 77, *77*; during COVID-19, 152; under Cutchin, 24; under Hood, *153*; injuries, 10–11; under Nutt, *85*, 85–86; at Roy Stewart Stadium, 65 (*see also* Roy Stewart Stadium); scholarships for, 51; under Stewart, *23*, 23–24. *See also individual players*

Foreign Students Organization, 43, 78

Freakers Ball, *76*

Friends of Pinnacle, *150*

Frog Hop, *67*, 67–68

Fulks, Joe, 30, 38–39, *39*

fundraising for charities, 73, *73*, *75*, 80–81, 98

Furgerson, Bill, 49

Fuze (underground newspaper), 62, *62*

Gamma Delta, 32

Garfield, Gene, 83, *83*

Garrett, Bill, 30

Gene W. Ray Center for Racer Basketball, 91, 119

Gentry, Jeff, 155

G.I. Bill (Servicemen's Readjustment Act, 1944), 30, 36

golf, 52, 56, 71, *73*, 74, 91, *121*

Graduate School, 43

Graves, Gilbert, 10–11, *11*

Graves, Wildy H., 10–11

Great Beginnings Racer Life event, *153*

Great Depression, 25, 28–29, 42

Great Recession (2008), 122

Greek life, 55, 57. *See also individual fraternities and sororities*

Green, Jeff, *95*

Gudauskas, Pete ("The Toe"), 29–30, *34*, 35

Guess, Susan, 123, *146*

Guffey, Amber, 91, *104*, 104–5

Hall, Charles Edward, *138*

Hampton, Jenean, 123

Hancock, Hunter, 63

Hancock Biological Station, 63, *63*

Hanging of the Green, 55, *69*

Harry Lee Waterfield Student Union Building, 42

Haseldon, Jane, *36*, 36–37

Head, Nita, 56

Health Building. *See* John W. Carr Hall

Helm, Emma J., 11

Henley, Melvin, 132, 134, *134*, *150*

Henley, Rita, 132, *134*, *150*

Heritage Hall, *112*

Hester, Cleo Gillis, *19*

Hester Hall, *19*, 80

Hewitt, Raymond ("Buddy"), 52, *52*

Hicks, Morgan, 91, 101, *101*

Higginson, Bonnie, *107*, 107–8

Hodges, Harlan, *45*

Hogancamp, Thomas, 44–45, *45*

Hoke, Anne Wrather, 33

Hold Thy Banner High campaign, *95*, 122–23, 127–28, 132

Holland, Mary Ford, 43, 48, *48*

Hollis C. Franklin Residential Hall, 123

Homecoming, *22*

Honors College, 123
Hood, Dean, *153*
Hortin, L. J., 18–19, *19*
Hughes, Bob, 155
Hughes, Eugene and Ruth, 26
Hunt, Jill, *154*
Hussein, Saddam, 148–49
Hut (restaurant), 26, *26*, 50, *50*
Hutchinson, James H., 9
Hutson, Cindy and Sue, 91
Hutson, Nicholas, 91
Hutson family, 91, *136*
Hutson Harvest Gala, 90–91, *115*
Hutson School of Agriculture, 75, 91, 114–15, *115*, 123

ice storm (2009), 106, *106*
Inca empire, 47
Industrial Arts Building, 41, *41*
industrial arts program, 41
Insight '71 lecture series, *62*, 62–63
integration of colleges and universities, 43, 48–50
International Student Organization (ISO), 78, *78*
Internet age, 70, 72, 119

Jackson, Dennis, 43, *48*, 48–49
Jackson, Karen, 123, 128, *146*, 155
Jackson, Robert L, *95*, 123, 126, 128, 132, *133*, *146*
Jackson State College (Mississippi), 58
Janice F. and Richard F. Weaver Student-Athlete Academic Scholarship, 79
Jesse D. Jones Chemistry Building, 128
Jesse D. Jones College of Science, Engineering and Technology, 123, 128
Jesse L. Jones Family Clock Tower, 127, *128–30*, *158*
Jim Crow racial segregation, 48
John H. Shroat and James H. Reid Intramural Complex, 121
Johnson, Anna Mayrell, 29, *36*, 36–37, 56
Johnson, Charles and Marlene, *153*
Johnson, Stewart, 50
John W. Carr Hall (*formerly* Health Building), 21, 31, *31*, *152*
Jones, Brereton, *95*
Jones, Deb, *129*
Jones, Jesse D., 91, 122–23, 127–28, *128–29*, *134*
Jones, Ronald ("Popeye"), 71, 82–83, *83*
Jones, Seth and Caleb, 83
Jones College of Science, Engineering and Technology, 119
Joseph and Joseph, 7, 8
J. Rogers Badgett Foundation, 138

Kelly, Don, *95*
Kemp, Dan, *133*
Kennedy, Billy, 108
Kent State University (Ohio), 58
Kentucky State College for Negroes (Frankfort), 43
Keys, Arlene France, 43
King, W. Fain, 75
Koehler-Church, Kim, 84, *84*
Koffman, Irby, 9
Korean War, 61
Korir, Wesley, *100*
Kunstler, William, *62*, 62–63

Labor Day, 18
Lambda Chi Alpha, 55, 63, *63*
Lambda Eta, 63
Land Between the Lakes National Recreation Area, 19
Lee Clark College, 9
Liberal Arts Building, 27
Live from Here (formerly *A Prairie Home Companion*), 99
Long, Jewuan, *111*
Lovett, Laurine Wells, *10*, 21
Lovett, Wells T., 21
Lovett Auditorium (MSU): Charles and Marlene Johnson Lobby, 123, *153*; interior view, *20*; live entertainment at, 55; planning for, 5; size of, 20–21
Lovett Live!, 90, *107*
Lowry, Clifton ("C. S."), 16, *16*
Lowry Library Annex, 16, 68
Luther, Cal, 50, *50*

March of Dimes, 98
Marine Corps, 30, 39
Marshall, George C., 38
Martin, Jeff, 80
Marvin College (Hickman County, Ky.), 2
Mason, Ora Kress, 44, *44*
Mason, William, 44
Mason Hall, 44
Mason Memorial Hospital School of Nursing, 43–44, *44*
Max Carman Outstanding Teacher Award, 19
May Day, 17–18, *18*
McGaughey, Bob ("Doc"), 53, *53*
McMahon, Matt, 108, 142–43
McRaven, Claude ("Mac"), 29, *31*, 148–49
McRaven, William H., 148–49, *149*
Miles, Isacc, *109*
military science, 61–62
Milkman, Velvet, 91, *121*
Miller, Frances, 74

Miller, L. D., 74
Miller, Robert O., 63
Miller, Tim, *95*, 123, 126, *127*
Miller Memorial Golf Course, 71, *73*, 74
Mills, Eunice, 82, *82*
Mills, Marvin D., Sr., 82, *82*
Mills Emerging Scholars, *82*
Minority Student Affairs (MSA), 76–77, *77*
Miss Black and Gold, 76, *76*
Mississippi Valley Conference, 25
Mofield, Ray, *41*, 59
Moon Buggy, 45
Morant, Ja, 140, 142–43, *143–45*
Morgan, Jeanie, *146*
Morris, Edward Craig, 47, *47*
Moss, Mary W., 9
MSU-TV, *65*
Murphey, Garland, 9
Murray (Kentucky), 2, 64
Murray, Gene, 55
Murray, John L., 8
Murray State Art Auction, 61
Murray State News (formerly *College News*), 11, 14, *14*, 62
Murray State Normal School (*later* Murray State Normal School and Teachers College): Administration Building, 4, 9, *10*; architectural design of, 7, 8; Auditorium, 5 (*see also* Lovett Auditorium); board of regents for, 9–10, *10*, 63–65; under Carr, 4, 6–8; Classroom Building, 5 (*see also* Wilson Hall); clubs and societies at, 11; construction of, 3; culture/values of, 4; Depression-era financial struggles of, 28–30; dormitories at, 9, *16*, *51* (*see also* Ordway Hall; Wells Hall); enrollment at, postwar, 42; enrollment at, wartime, 29–30; evolution into a university (*see* Murray State University); first Black instructors/professors, 55, 59, *59*; first faculty members, 9; first seniors and graduates, 11, *13*; first students, 4; founding of, 3; funding for, 3; growth of, 4–6, 40–42, 54; integration of, 43, 48–50, 55; Library, 5, 21 (*see also* Pogue Library); the quad, *25*; reorganization into colleges, 54; reorganization into schools, 43; temporary classrooms for, 4; Wells Hall, 5
Murray State University (MSU; *formerly* Murray State Teachers College; *formerly* Murray State Normal School): alumni, number of, x; Black enrollment/retention, 76; board of regents for, 126, *154*; centennial celebration of, 126; degree programs, number of, x; first woman president, 70, 73; funding for, *154*; growth of, 68, 71; size of, x; stature of, x; university status, elevation to, *55*; website of, 71. *See also* Murray State Normal School
Murray State University Foundation, x, 35, 56

NASA, 45
Nash, William G., 35, *35*
Nash House, 35, *35*
National Public Radio, 59
National Youth Administration (NYA), 29
Naval Pre-Flight Preparatory Training Unit, 30, 36, *36*
NCAA, 66–67
New Murray Hotel, *6*
newspapers, underground, 62, *62*
Newton, Steve, *80*
New York Presbyterian Hospital, *156*
Nickel Creek, 98–99
normal schools, 3–8, 16. *See also specific schools*
nursing program, 44
Nutt, Houston, *85*, 85–86
NYA (National Youth Administration), 29

Oakhurst (*formerly* Edgewood), 15, *15*, *146*
Oakley, Hugh, 40–41, *41*
Obama, Barack, 108
Office of Alumni Relations, 81
Office of Development, 94, *112*
Office of Multicultural Initiatives, Student Leadership and Inclusive Excellence, 77
Officer, Tom, 50
Ohio Valley Conference. *See* OVC
Onionhead, 34
Ordway Hall, 21–22, *22*, 69
OVC (Ohio Valley Conference), *45*, 105; founding of, 23; Hall of Fame, 23; integration of, 43, 48–49

Paducah Community College (*now* West Kentucky Community and Technical College), 73
pandemic. *See* COVID-19 pandemic
Paul Bunyan Day, 55, 57, *57*
Payne, Cameron, 140, *141*
Pennington, Stella, 9
Perry, Willie Earl, 43
Phillips, Richard, 148–49
Phi Mu Alpha, 32
Pi Kappa Alpha, 75
Pogue, Forrest C., 16, 29, *37*, 38
Pogue Library (MSU), 5, 21, *21*, *37*–38, 53, 56
Porter, Michael and Lana, *150*
Prairie Home Companion, A (now *Live from Here*), 99
Price Doyle Fine Arts Building, 24, 29, 54, 59–61

Pritchett, Jerry Sue, 55, 58, *58*
Prohibition, 63
Prohm, Steve, 108, 114
Pullen, Mabel, 114
Pullen, Stanley, 114
Pullen Farm, 114
Punch Brothers, 99
Purcell, Bennie, 105, *105*
Purcell, Mel, 105, *105*
Purchase Area (Kentucky), 2–3

Racer Arena, 46, *46*, 55, 94
Racer Band, 60, *60*, 148
Racer Live Productions, *107*
Racer One, 55, 67, *67*
Racer One statue, *150*
Racers (MSU athletic teams), 46. *See also individual*
    sports and athletes
Radio City Music Hall, *138*
Rainey T. Wells statue, *93*, 155
Ray, Gene W., 91, 119, *119*
Ray, Taffin, 119
Reagan, Johnny, 46, 52, *52*, 66–67, 71, 84–85
recessions, 56, 70, 122
Reelfoot Lake State Park, *20*
regional campuses, 115, *117*, 138
Regional Special Events Center (RSEC). *See* CFSB
    Center
Residential College system, 72, 96, 98
Rhoads, Jerry, 126, *154*
Rhoads, McHenry, *10*
Richmond, James, 28–30, *30*, 36, 40
Riddle, Hal, 29, 34, *34*
Riggins, Mark, 66, *66*
Riggins, Tammie, 66
Robbins, Kris and Lori, *150*
Robert Johnson Theatre, *60*, 60–61
Robertson, Don, 155
Robinson, Jackie, 48
Rock-A-Thon, 73, *73*
Roosevelt, Franklin, 29–30, 36
Rose, Jack and Janice, *150*, *152*
ROTC (Reserve Officers' Training Corps), *45*,
    45–46, 61–62
Rowlett, Dew Drop Brumley, 25, *25*, 56
Roy Stewart Stadium, 11, 23, 55, *65*
RSEC. *See* CFSB Center
Rueter, Kirk ("Woody"), 71, 84–85, *85*
Russell, Johny B., *45*, 45

Saal, Kevin, *153*
Samuel, Heather, 84, *84*
Shield, The (yearbook), 11, *14*

shield logo, x, 8
Shoe Tree, 43, 52, *53*
Shroat, Jerry and Betsy, 91, *120*, 120–21
Sigma Alpha Iota, 32, 51
Sigma Chi, 55, 57
Sigma Sigma Sigma (Tri Sigma), 81, *81*
Simmons, Margaret, 56–57, *57*
sit-ins, 49, 58
Smith, Brinda, 37, 56, *56*
Smith, Dennis and June, *150*
Smith, E. H., 9, *9*
Smith, Jordan, 155
Smith, Mary Johnson, 37, 56
Smith, Sheila, 78, *78*
Smith-Johnson Genealogy and History Room, 37,
    56
soccer, 24, 56, 91, 140, *142*
Sock and Buskin Club, 14, *14*
Sommer, Stacy, 71
Southeastern Conference, 48
Sparks, Harry, 58, *58*, 64
Spring, Joel, x
Spurgin, Pat, 71, 77, *77*
Stable Doors, 68
Staton, Joe, 62, *62*
Stause, Chrishell, 91, 94, 99, *99*
Stewart, Roy, *23*, 23–25, 50
Stokes, Tom, *10*
Stout, Alan, *129*
Streety, Frank, *50*
Stroup, Kala, 70, 72, *72*–73, 79
Student Alumni Association, 80
Student Government Association (SGA), 19,
    62–63
study abroad programs, 72, *84*
Susan E. Bauernfeind Student Recreation and
    Wellness Center, *103*, 104

Tammie Riggins Memorial Scholarship, 66
Tapp, Gondee, *13*
Taste of the Arts, 90, 94, 106, *106*, *120*
teaching exchange programs, 72
Teeter for Tots, 75
tennis, 56, 105
Tent City, 71, *78*, 81, *81*
Tharpe, Don, *147*
theatre, 14, *14*, 34, *60*, 60–61, 71. *See also* Campus
    Lights
Thile, Chris, 91, 98–99, *99*
Thile, Scott, 98
Thomas, Danero, 108
Thomas, Prentice, *10*
Thornton, Jerry Sue Pritchett, 55, 58, *58*

Thoroughbreds (MSU athletic teams), 6, 21, 23–25, *24–25*, 38–39, 46, 52. *See also individual sports and athletes*
Titan Corporation, 119
Title IX (Education Amendments Act, 1972), 56
Todd, Tim, *147*, 155
Training School Institute (*later* University School), 16–17, *17–18*
Tri Sigma, 71
Truman, Harry, 37, 48

Universität Regensburg (Bavaria), 72, *84*
University of Cambridge (England), 72
University of Louisville, 23
University of Oxford (England), 72
University School (*formerly* Training School Institute), 16–17, *17–18*
Upshaw, W. D., 11
US Navy, 29
US Navy Nurse Corps, 36

Valentine, Bob, 66, *66*
Vietnam War, 53, 55–56, 58
Violet Cactus, 67, *67*
Vitale, Dick, *97*
Volleybash, 81, *81*

Walker, Belle, 9
Wallace Village (Colorado), 57
Ward, Jack and Millie, 26
Waterfield, Harry Lee, 68, *68*
Waterfield Library, 68, *68*
Waterfield Student Union Building, 68
Watermelon Bust, 63, *63*
Watkins, Sara and Sean, 98–99
WAVES (Women Accepted for Volunteer Emergency Service), 36–37
Weaver, Dick, 79
Weaver, Jan, 79, *79*
Weaver Center, 79
Wells, Geneve, 60
Wells, Rainey T., *6*; background of, 6; children and grandchildren of, 6, 15, 21, 60; Edgewood home of, 15, *15*; education promoted by, 2, 6; influence of, 126; as a lawyer, 6–7; as Murray State Normal School president, 6; normal-school bid by, 3, 5–6; normal school founded by, x, 3–4, 28; as a politician, 6; statue of, *93*, *155*; working relationship with Carr, 7
Wells, Tennie Daniel, 6, 21
Wells Hall (MSU), 5, *16*, 25
Western Baptist Hospital (Paducah, Ky.), 71

Western Kentucky State Normal School (Bowling Green, Ky.), 3
Western Kentucky University, 23
West Kentucky Livestock and Exposition Center (*later* William "Bill" Cherry Agricultural Exposition Center), 67, *67*
White, Carrie Allison, *24*, 25
Wickliffe Mounds (Mississippi), 71, 75, *75*
Wilson, James, *10*, 14
Wilson, Woodrow, 11
Wilson Hall, 5, *9*, *13*, 14, *15*, 16, 59
Wilsonian Society, 11, *12*
Winslow Cafeteria, *52*
Withers, Harriet, 140, *142*
WKMS radio, 14, 59
women's athletics: basketball, *24–25*, 25, 46, 56, 78, *78*, 91; coaches, 56, 56–57; cross-country, 56; equal opportunities for women, 55–56; expansion of, 55; football, *87*; golf, 56, 91, *121*; soccer, 24, 91; softball, 56, 91; tennis, 56; track and field, 56, 72, *84*; volleyball, 46, *56*. *See also individual athletes*
women's rights movement, 47, 58
Women's Self-Government Association, 11
Women's Student Government Association, 55
Woods, Ralph H.: *Fifty Years of Progress*, x; as MSU president, 40, *41*, 48, 50, 61
Woods Park, *149*
Works Progress Administration, 29
World War II: D-Day, 30; economic boom following, 42; MSU faculty members' military service in, 38; MSU students' military service in, 29–30, 34, 36–37, 39, *40*; Pearl Harbor attack, 32; rationing during, *40*; US entry into, 29
WPAD radio, *41*
Wrather, Marvin ("M. O."), 9, 33, *33*, 50
Wrather Hall (*formerly* Administration Building), x, 4, 9, *10*, 33
Wrather West Kentucky Museum, 4, 9, *10*
www.mursuky.edu, 71

Zacharias, Alan, 75
Zeta Omicron, 76, 98